# tapasBar

easy snacks from the mediterranean

**THE AUSTRALIAN**
# Women's Weekly

# contents

Tapas have been readily adopted by Australians as they really suit our lifestyle. Tapas has become the generic word for small portions of exciting flavoursome food – served both hot and cold – from lunchtime onwards. Traditionally, tapas are served in bars, late at night in Spain, mezze hail from Greece, North Africa and the Middle East and antipasto mainly comes from Italy.

*Pamela Clark*
Food Director

# tapas

olives

## martini olives

Rinse and drain 370ml can anchovy-stuffed green manzanilla olives; combine in medium bowl with 1 tablespoon finely chopped fresh rosemary, 4 bay leaves, 1 tablespoon extra dry vermouth, 1 tablespoon gin and ½ cup olive oil. Cover, refrigerate overnight or up to one week. Serve olives with crusty bread.

---

**prep** *15 minutes*
*(+ refrigeration)* **serves** *8*
**nutritional count per serving**
*17.3g total fat (2.5g saturated fat);*
*711kJ (170 cal); 0.7g carbohydrate;*
*0.3g protein; 2.9g fibre*

**Spanish anchovy-stuffed green manzanilla olives can be found at specialty food stores.**

## fennel, mint and orange olives

Combine 1 cup seeded ligurian olives, 1 trimmed, thinly sliced baby fennel bulb, ½ cup fresh mint leaves, 2 tablespoons finely grated orange rind, 1 teaspoon black peppercorns and 1½ cups olive oil in medium bowl. Cover, refrigerate overnight or up to one week.

---

**prep time** *15 minutes*
*(+ refrigeration)* **serves** *8*
**nutritional count per serving**
*42.9g total fat (6.1g saturated fat);*
*1689kJ (404 cal); 5.2g carbohydrate;*
*0.4g protein; 0.9g fibre*

**Ligurian olives are medium-sized black olives found in specialty food stores; kalamata or any other black olives can be substituted.**

### peri-peri olives

Combine 1¼ cups seeded kalamata olives, 1 tablespoon finely grated lemon rind, 2 halved fresh small red thai chillies, 2 garlic cloves, ¼ cup red wine vinegar and ¾ cup olive oil in medium bowl. Cover, refrigerate overnight or up to 1 week.

prep *15 minutes*
*(+ refrigeration)* serves *8*
**nutritional count per serving**
*21.6g total fat (3.1g saturated fat);*
*899kJ (215 cal); 5.6g carbohydrate;*
*0.2g protein; 0.5g fibre*

### olives with caperberries and sherry vinegar

Combine 1¼ cups sicilian green olives, 1 cup rinsed drained caperberries, 5 sprigs fresh lemon thyme, ¼ cup sherry vinegar and ¾ cup olive oil in medium bowl. Cover, refrigerate overnight or up to 1 week.

prep time *15 minutes*
*(+ refrigeration)* serves *8*
**nutritional count per serving**
*21.6g total fat (3.1g saturated fat);*
*932kJ (223 cal); 7.3g carbohydrate;*
*0.3g protein; 0.6g fibre*

### olives with saffron and cheese

Combine 1 cup capsicum-stuffed green olives, 2 thinly sliced garlic cloves, 1⅓ cups coarsely chopped semi-hard sheep-milk cheese, ½ teaspoon saffron threads and 1 cup olive oil in medium bowl. Cover, refrigerate overnight or up to 1 week.

prep time *15 minutes*
*(+ refrigeration)* serves *8*
**nutritional count per serving**
*37.5g total fat (9g saturated fat);*
*1530kJ (366 cal); 0.5g carbohydrate;*
*7.4 g protein; 1.6g fibre*

**Sheep-milk cheese can be found in specialty food stores. It can be substituted with other firm cheeses such as spanish goats cheese, provolone or mozzarella.**

bites

## caramelised tomato and ham bites

Cook 2 finely chopped shallots in heated oiled medium frying pan until soft. Add 250g halved cherry tomatoes; cook 5 minutes. Add ¼ cup balsamic vinegar and 1 tablespoon brown sugar; cook, stirring occasionally, until thickened. Cut 1 brioche loaf into 16 slices; cut 32 x 6.5cm rounds from slices. Top half the slices with 2 cups finely grated semi-hard sheep-milk cheese; grill until cheese melts. Toast remaining rounds until golden. Divide 185g thinly sliced double smoked leg ham among toast rounds; top each with caramelised tomatoes, top with remaining toasts. Serve warm.

prep + cook time *40 minutes* makes 16
nutritional count per bite
*7.5g total fat (4.1g saturated fat);*
*644kJ (154 cal); 12.7g carbohydrate;*
*8.4g protein; 0.7g fibre*

## prawn and caper sandwiches

Combine 300g cooked, shelled, finely chopped prawns, ¼ cup rinsed drained, finely chopped capers, 1 cup mayonnaise, 1 teaspoon sweet paprika, ¼ cup finely chopped fresh flat-leaf parsley and 1 crushed garlic clove in medium bowl. Divide prawn mixture between 9 slices of white bread; top with another 9 slices bread. Trim crusts; cut each sandwich into four triangles.

prep time *30 minutes* makes *36*
nutritional count per triangle
*2.6g total fat (0.3g saturated fat);*
*255kJ (61 cal); 7g carbohydrate;*
*2.1g protein; 0.4g fibre*

## asparagus and coppa salad bites

Boil, steam or microwave 170g trimmed asparagus, drain. Finely chop asparagus; combine with 1 finely chopped small red onion, 2 tablespoons finely chopped fresh basil, 2 teaspoons red wine vinegar and 2 tablespoons olive oil in medium bowl. Split 10 mini croissants in half. Divide 200g thinly sliced coppa among half the croissants; top with asparagus mixture, then remaining croissant halves. Serve at room temperature.

prep time *15 minutes* makes *10*
nutritional count per bite
*11.4g total fat (4.6g saturated fat); 744kJ (178 cal); 11.5g carbohydrate; 6.9g protein; 1.1g fibre*

## chicken, almond and tarragon mini rolls

Combine 200g cooked finely shredded chicken breast fillet, ⅓ cup finely chopped fresh tarragon, ¼ cup roasted slivered almonds, 1 trimmed finely chopped celery stalk, 3 finely chopped green onions and ⅓ cup mayonnaise in medium bowl. Make a cut in tops of 12 mini bread rolls. Spoon chicken mixture into bread rolls.

prep time *20 minutes* makes *12*
nutritional count per roll
*5.7g total fat (0.7g saturated fat); 660kJ (158 cal); 17.5g carbohydrate; 8.2g protein; 1.7g fibre*

**Chicken mixture can be made one day ahead; keep, covered, in the refrigerator.**

## blue cheese and fig bites

Process ⅓ cup roasted slivered almonds with 2 coarsely chopped green onions, 1 cup loosely packed fresh mint leaves, ⅓ cup olive oil and 1 tablespoon lemon juice until smooth. Halve 1 long turkish loaf lengthways; cut each half lengthways into 3 fingers then cut fingers into four crossways to get 24 slices. Toast bread under hot grill. Spread almond mixture on half the toasts; top with 200g thinly sliced semi-dried figs and 100g thinly sliced blue cheese. Top with remaining toast; serve warm.

prep + cook time *20 minutes* makes *12*
nutritional count per bite
*11.9g total fat (2.9g saturated fat); 1012kJ (242 cal); 25.5g carbohydrate; 6.2g protein; 3.9g fibre*

9

# garlic and paprika char-grilled prawns

12 uncooked medium king prawns (540g)
1 medium red capsicum (200g),
    chopped coarsely
⅓ cup (80ml) olive oil
2 cloves garlic, crushed
1 teaspoon smoked paprika

1   Shell and devein prawns, leaving tails intact.
2   Combine prawns, capsicum, oil, garlic and paprika in medium bowl.
3   Cook capsicum on heated grill plate until browned both sides. Add prawns towards the end of capsicum cooking time; cook, turning, until prawns are changed in colour.
4   Serve with lemon wedges, if you like.

prep + cook time *30 minutes* serves *6*
nutritional count per serving  *12.5g total fat (1.8g saturated fat); 652kJ (156 cal); 1.2g carbohydrate; 9.7g protein; 0.5g fibre*

# prawns with fresh tomato sauce

12 uncooked medium king prawns (540g)
2 tablespoons olive oil
4 cloves garlic, sliced thinly
4 medium vine-ripened tomatoes (420g),
    chopped coarsely
2 teaspoons red wine vinegar
1 tablespoon coarsely chopped fresh
    flat-leaf parsley

Shell and devein prawns, leaving tails intact.
Heat oil in large frying pan; cook garlic until
browned lightly. Add tomato; cook, uncovered,
stirring occasionally, about 5 minutes. Add
prawns and vinegar; cook until prawns change
colour. Stir in parsley.
    Serve with crusty bread.

# soft-shell crabs with green onion aïoli

½ cup (100g) rice flour
1 teaspoon dried chilli flakes
2 teaspoons sea salt
8 uncooked small soft-shell crabs (500g)
vegetable oil, for deep frying
1 cup loosely packed fresh basil leaves
**green onion aïoli**
¾ cup (225g) mayonnaise
2 green onions, sliced finely
1 clove garlic, crushed
1 tablespoon lemon juice

**1** Make green onion aïoli.
**2** Combine flour, chilli and salt in medium bowl.
**3** Clean crabs; pat dry then cut into quarters. Coat crabs with flour mixture; shake away excess.
**4** Heat oil in large saucepan; deep-fry basil about 30 seconds or until crisp. Drain on absorbent paper. Deep-fry crabs, in batches, until browned lightly. Drain on absorbent paper. Serve with basil and aïoli.
**green onion aïoli** Combine ingredients in small bowl.

**prep + cook time** *30 minutes* **serves** *8*
**nutritional count per serving** *13g total fat (1.5g saturated fat); 920kJ (220 cal); 16.7g carbohydrate; 9g protein; 0.6g fibre*

# grilled mussels with prosciutto

20 small black mussels (500g)
2 cups (500ml) water
80g butter, softened
50g thinly sliced prosciutto, chopped finely
1 clove garlic, crushed
2 green onions, chopped finely

**1** Scrub mussels; remove beards. Bring the water to the boil in large saucepan. Add the mussels, cover; boil about 3 minutes or until mussels open (discard any that do not).
**2** Drain mussels; discard liquid. Break open shells; discard top shell. Loosen mussels from shells with a spoon; return mussels to shells, place in single layer on oven tray.
**3** Preheat grill.
**4** Combine butter, prosciutto, garlic and onion in small bowl.
**5** Divide butter mixture over mussels; grill about 3 minutes or until browned lightly.

**prep + cook time** *30 minutes* **serves** *4*
**nutritional count per serving** *17.6g total fat (11.2g saturated fat); 773kJ (185 cal); 1.8g carbohydrate; 5.5g protein; 0.2g fibre*

# cod and olive fritters

650g salted cod fillet, skin on
3 medium potatoes (600g), halved
1 tablespoon olive oil
1 medium brown onion (150g), chopped finely
2 cloves garlic, crushed
¼ cup finely chopped fresh flat-leaf parsley
½ cup (60g) seeded green olives, chopped finely
1 egg
vegetable oil, for deep-frying

**1** Rinse fish under cold water to remove excess salt. Place fish in large bowl, cover with cold water; refrigerate, covered, overnight, changing the water three or four times. Drain fish; discard water.

**2** Place fish in large saucepan, cover with cold water; bring to the boil uncovered. Reduce heat, simmer, covered, 5 minutes. Drain fish, discard water; remove skin and bones then flake fish.

**3** Boil, steam or microwave potato until tender; drain. Roughly mash potato in large bowl.

**4** Meanwhile, heat olive oil in large frying pan; cook onion and garlic, stirring, until onion softens.

**5** Combine fish, onion mixture, parsley, olives and egg with potato; mix well.

**6** Roll level tablespoons of fish mixture into balls, place on baking-paper-lined tray; refrigerate 30 minutes.

**7** Heat vegetable oil in deep medium saucepan; deep-fry fritters, in batches, until browned lightly and heated through. Drain on absorbent paper.

**prep + cook time** *1 hour 30 minutes (+ refrigeration)* **makes** *40*
**nutritional count per fritter** *2.6g total fat (0.4g saturated fat); 196kJ (47 cal); 47.4g carbohydrate; 3.6g protein; 0.3g fibre*

Salted cod, also known as salt cod, baccalà, bacalhau, bacalao and morue, is available from Italian, Spanish and Portuguese delicatessens and some speciality food stores. It needs to be de-salted and rehydrated before use.

# pan-seared scallops with anchovy butter

2 teaspoons olive oil
12 scallops (300g), roe removed
30g butter
3 drained anchovy fillets
2 cloves garlic, crushed
2 teaspoons lemon juice
1 tablespoon finely chopped fresh chives

**1** Heat oil in large frying pan; cook scallops, both sides, until browned lightly. Remove from pan; cover to keep warm.

**2** Add butter, anchovies and garlic to pan; cook, stirring, until garlic is browned lightly. Return scallops to pan with juice; cook until scallops are heated through. Serve scallops drizzled with anchovy butter and sprinkled with chives.

**prep + cook time** *15 minutes* **serves 4**
**nutritional count per serving** *9.1g total fat (4.8g saturated fat); 514kJ (123 cal); 0.8g carbohydrate; 9.6g protein; 0.3g fibre*

# saffron and brandy squid

4 small cleaned squid hoods (300g),
   sliced thinly
2 cloves garlic, crushed
pinch saffron threads
2 teaspoons hot water
1 tablespoon olive oil
2 tablespoons brandy
100g baby spinach leaves

1  Combine squid and garlic in medium bowl.
2  Place saffron in small dish; stir in the water.
3  Heat oil in large frying pan; cook squid until browned lightly, remove from pan.
4  Add brandy to pan; cook about 30 seconds or until brandy has almost evaporated.
5  Add spinach and saffron to pan; cook, stirring, until spinach is wilted. Return squid to pan; mix gently. Serve immediately.

prep + cook time *10 minutes*  serves 4
nutritional count per serving  *5.6g total fat
(1g saturated fat); 527kJ (126 cal);
0.3g carbohydrate; 13.2g protein; 0.9g fibre*

# octopus braised with red wine and fennel

1 tablespoon olive oil
1 medium brown onion (150g), chopped finely
2 cloves garlic, crushed
2 baby fennel bulbs (260g), trimmed,
    chopped coarsely
5 medium vine-ripened tomatoes (560g),
    chopped coarsely
3 bay leaves
1 teaspoon dried chilli flakes
680g whole octopus
⅔ cup (160ml) dry red wine
2 tablespoons finely chopped fresh
    flat-leaf parsley

**1**  Preheat oven to 200°C/180°C fan-forced.
**2**  Heat oil in large frying pan; cook onion and garlic, stirring, until onion softens. Add fennel; cook, stirring, 5 minutes. Add tomato, bay leaves and chilli; cook, stirring occasionally, about 10 minutes or until mixture thickens and fennel is softened.
**3**  Combine fennel mixture, octopus and wine in medium baking dish; bake, covered, about 45 minutes. Uncover; bake about 40 minutes or until octopus is tender and browned lightly.
**4**  Cut octopus into bite-sized pieces. Stir in parsley. Serve with crusty bread, if you like.

**prep + cook time** *2 hours*  **serves** *8*
**nutritional count per serving**  *3g total fat (0.3g saturated fat); 493kJ (118 cal); 3.1g carbohydrate; 15.2g protein; 1.8g fibre*

# potato, dill and prawn tortilla

30g butter
2 teaspoons olive oil
2 medium potatoes (400g), chopped finely
1 medium brown onion (150g), chopped finely
12 uncooked medium king prawns (540g)
6 eggs
2 tablespoons sour cream
2 tablespoons finely chopped fresh dill

**1** Preheat oven to 200°C/180°C fan-forced.
**2** Heat butter and oil in medium frying pan; cook potato, stirring occasionally, 5 minutes. Add onion; cook, stirring occasionally, until potato is browned and tender.
**3** Meanwhile, shell and devein prawns; add to pan with potato. Cook until prawns change colour.
**4** Whisk eggs with sour cream in medium bowl until smooth; stir in dill. Pour mixture into pan; stir gently. Cook tortilla over low heat, about 10 minutes or until bottom sets. Wrap pan handle in foil; place pan in oven. Cook tortilla, uncovered, about 15 minutes or until tortilla is set and browned.
**5** Stand tortilla 10 minutes before cutting into bite size pieces; serve warm.

**prep + cook time** *45 minutes* **serves** *10*
**nutritional count per serving** *8.3g total fat (3.8g saturated fat); 589kJ (141 cal); 5.5g carbohydrate; 10.7g protein; 0.8g fibre*

# chicken, raisin and pine nut empanadas

1 litre (4 cups) water
1 chicken breast fillet (200g)
2 teaspoons olive oil
1 small brown onion (80g), chopped finely
2 cloves garlic, crushed
½ can (205g) crushed tomatoes
1 bay leaf
¼ teaspoon dried chilli flakes
2 tablespoons raisins, chopped coarsely
2 tablespoons pine nuts, roasted
½ teaspoon ground cinnamon
2 tablespoons finely chopped fresh
   flat-leaf parsley
1 egg

**pastry**

1⅔ cups (250g) plain flour
150g cold butter, chopped
1 egg
1 tablespoon cold water

1  Bring the water to the boil in medium saucepan; add chicken, return to the boil. Reduce heat; simmer, covered, about 10 minutes or until chicken is cooked through. Cool chicken in poaching liquid 10 minutes. Remove chicken from pan; discard poaching liquid. Shred chicken finely.

2  Heat oil in medium frying pan; cook onion and garlic, stirring, until onion softens. Add undrained tomato, bay leaf and chilli; cook, stirring occasionally, about 5 minutes or until mixture thickens.

3  Add chicken, raisins, nuts and cinnamon to tomato mixture; stir until heated through. Stir in parsley. Cool mixture, covered, in the refrigerator.

4  Meanwhile, make pastry.
5  Preheat oven to 200°C/180°C fan-forced.
6  Roll one pastry half between sheets of baking paper until 2mm thick; using 10cm-round cutter, cut 10 rounds from pastry.
7  Place 1 level tablespoon of chicken mixture in centre of each round; fold round in half to enclose filling, pinching edges to seal. Press around edges of empanadas with a fork. Repeat with remaining pastry half and chicken mixture to make a total of 20 empanadas, re-rolling pastry scraps as required.
8  Place empanadas on baking-paper-lined oven trays; brush with egg. Bake about 20 minutes or until browned lightly.

**pastry** Process flour and butter until crumbly. Add egg and the water; process until mixture comes together. Knead dough on floured surface until smooth. Divide pastry in half, enclose in plastic wrap; refrigerate 30 minutes.

**prep + cook time** *2 hours*
*(+ refrigeration)* **makes** *20*
**nutritional count per empanada** *8.9g total fat (4.5g saturated fat); 594kJ (142 cal); 10.6g carbohydrate; 4.6g protein; 0.9g fibre*

**Chicken filling can be made one day ahead. Pastry can be made one week ahead; keep in the freezer until ready to use.**

# lemon and chilli chicken skewers

400g chicken breast fillets, cut into 2cm pieces
2 chorizo (340g), cut into 2cm pieces
1 medium yellow capsicum (200g),
    cut into 2cm pieces
12 bay leaves
1 tablespoon finely grated lemon rind
1 tablespoon lemon juice
¼ cup (60ml) olive oil
2 cloves garlic, crushed
1 teaspoon dried chilli flakes
¼ cup finely chopped fresh flat-leaf parsley

1 Combine ingredients in large bowl; cover, refrigerate 30 minutes.
2 Thread chicken, chorizo, capsicum and bay leaves, alternately, onto skewers.
3 Cook skewers on heated oiled grill plate (or grill or barbecue) until chicken is cooked through and chorizo is browned lightly.

**prep + cook time** *30 minutes*
*(+ refrigeration)* **makes** *12*
**nutritional count per skewer** *15.3g total fat (4.4g saturated fat); 832kJ (199 cal); 1.3g carbohydrate; 14.3g protein; 0.4g fibre*

**Soak 12 bamboo skewers in water for at least an hour before using to prevent them from scorching during cooking.**

# sherry-glazed chicken livers

1 tablespoon olive oil
500g chicken livers, trimmed, sliced thinly
20g butter
2 shallots (50g), chopped finely
⅓ cup (80ml) dry sherry
½ cup (125ml) chicken stock
2 small long crusty bread rolls (120g),
    sliced into 6 slices each
30g watercress sprigs
1 teaspoon sherry vinegar

**1** Heat oil in large frying pan; add liver, stir over high heat about 1 minute or until liver is barely cooked. Remove from pan; cover to keep warm.
**2** Add butter and shallot to same pan; cook, stirring, until shallot softens.
**3** Add sherry to pan; simmer until liquid is reduced by half. Add stock; simmer until liquid is slightly thickened. Return liver to pan; stir until heated.
**4** Toast bread rolls lightly both sides.
**5** Spoon liver mixture over toast; sprinkle watercress with vinegar. Top toasts with watercress mixture.

**prep + cook time** *30 minutes*  **makes** *12*
**nutritional count per piece**  *4.9g total fat*
*(1.7g saturated fat); 464kJ (111 cal);*
*6.1g carbohydrate; 8.7g protein; 0.5g fibre*

# fennel and garlic roasted pork ribs

1 tablespoon fennel seeds
⅓ cup (90g) tomato paste
1 tablespoon brown sugar
¼ cup (60ml) sherry vinegar
4 cloves garlic, crushed
2 teaspoons smoked paprika
¼ cup (60ml) olive oil
2 x 500g racks pork spare ribs

**1** Combine seeds, paste, sugar, vinegar, garlic, paprika and oil in medium jug. Reserve ¼ cup of the marinade. Place pork in shallow dish, pour over marinade; turn pork to coat in marinade. Cover; refrigerate 1 hour.
**2** Preheat oven to 200°C/180°C fan-forced.
**3** Place pork on oiled wire rack over large baking dish; roast, uncovered, 30 minutes.
**4** Increase oven temperature to 220°C/200°C fan-forced. Brush pork with reserved marinade; roast about 20 minutes or until cooked through.
**5** Slice ribs between the bones; serve with lemon wedges, if you like.

**prep + cook** *time 1 hour*
*(+ refrigeration)* **serves** *6*
**nutritional count per serving** *15.2g total fat (3.3g saturated fat); 915kJ (219 cal); 3.9g carbohydrate; 16.5g protein; 1g fibre*

# artichoke and asparagus fritters with olive relish

170g asparagus, trimmed, chopped finely
280g jar artichokes in brine, drained,
    chopped finely
2 eggs
2 tablespoons finely chopped fresh mint
½ cup (40g) finely grated parmesan cheese
¼ cup (35g) self-raising flour
vegetable oil, for shallow frying
**olive relish**
½ cup (60g) seeded green olives, chopped finely
½ cup (60g) seeded black olives, chopped finely
¼ cup finely chopped fresh flat-leaf parsley
1 tablespoon finely chopped fresh chives
1 tablespoon olive oil
1 tablespoon lemon juice

**1**  Make olive relish.
**2**  Combine asparagus, artichoke, eggs, mint,
cheese and flour in medium bowl.
**3**  Heat oil in large frying pan; shallow-fry heaped
tablespoons of fritter mixture, in batches, until
browned all over and cooked through. Drain fritters
on absorbent paper; serve hot with olive relish.
**olive relish**  Combine ingredients in small bowl.

**prep + cook** *time 40 minutes*  makes *15*
**nutritional count per fritter**  *4.6g total fat
(1.2g saturated fat); 288kJ (69 cal);
3.8g carbohydrate; 2.9g protein; 0.8g fibre*

# veal meatballs with gazpacho salsa

1 tablespoon olive oil

1 large brown onion (200g), chopped finely

2 cloves garlic, crushed

500g veal mince

2 tablespoons finely chopped fresh oregano

1½ cups (120g) finely grated manchego cheese

1 cup (70g) stale breadcrumbs

1 egg

vegetable oil, for shallow-frying

**gazpacho salsa**

1 lebanese cucumber (130g), seeded,
    chopped finely

1 medium green capsicum (200g),
    chopped finely

½ small red onion (50g), chopped finely

1 small tomato (30g), seeded, chopped finely

2 tablespoons olive oil

1 tablespoon sherry vinegar

**1** Make gazpacho salsa.

**2** Heat olive oil in medium frying pan; cook onion and garlic, stirring, until onion softens. Cool 5 minutes.

**3** Combine onion mixture, veal, oregano, cheese, breadcrumbs and egg in large bowl. Roll rounded tablespoons of the veal mixture into balls.

**4** Heat vegetable oil in large frying pan; shallow-fry meatballs, in batches, until cooked through. Drain on absorbent paper. Serve hot with gazpacho salsa.

**gazpacho salsa** Combine ingredients in small bowl.

---

**prep + cook time** *50 minutes*  **makes** *40*
**nutritional count per meatball** *4.1g total fat
(1.1g saturated fat); 247kJ (59 cal);
1.7g carbohydrate; 3.7g protein; 0.3g fibre*

**Manchego cheese is a sharp, firm spanish cheese; it can be found in most specialty food stores. You can use parmesan cheese instead, if manchego is not available.**

# grilled eggplant with marjoram vinaigrette

1 large eggplant (500g),
   sliced into 5mm rounds
¼ cup (60ml) olive oil
1 small red onion (100g), sliced thinly
¼ cup (60ml) sherry vinegar
2 teaspoons caster sugar
2 tablespoons finely chopped fresh marjoram
½ cup (125ml) olive oil

1  Preheat oven to 200°C/180°C fan-forced.
2  Brush both sides of eggplant slices with oil; place, in single layer, on baking-paper-lined oven trays. Bake about 25 minutes, turning eggplant slices once, until browned lightly both sides.
3  Meanwhile, combine onion, vinegar, sugar, marjoram and oil in small bowl. Spoon onion mixture over eggplant.
4  Serve warm or at room temperature with crusty bread.

**prep + cook time** *50 minutes*  **serves** *6*
**nutritional count per serving**  *28.3g total fat (4g saturated fat); 1112kJ (278 cal); 4.6g carbohydrate; 1.2g protein; 2.2g fibre*

# anchovy and goats cheese baked mushrooms

20 large button mushrooms (400g)
1¾ cup (120g) stale breadcrumbs
120g soft goats cheese
¼ cup (60ml) olive oil
4 drained anchovy fillets, chopped finely
⅓ cup finely chopped fresh chives
1 cup (250ml) chicken stock

**1** Preheat oven to 200°C/180°C fan-forced.
**2** Remove and discard stems from mushrooms; place mushroom caps, in single layer, in medium baking dish.
**3** Combine breadcrumbs, cheese, oil, anchovy and chives in medium bowl. Stuff mushrooms with mixture.
**4** Add stock to baking dish; bake, uncovered, about 15 minutes or until mushrooms are browned lightly.

**prep + cook time** *40 minutes* **makes** *20*
**nutritional count per mushroom** *4.1g total fat
(1.1g saturated fat); 276kJ (66 cal);
4.3g carbohydrate; 2.7g protein; 0.8g fibre*

# broad beans and thyme

600g frozen broad beans, thawed
10g butter
2 shallots (50g), chopped finely
150g speck, chopped finely
1 tablespoon fresh thyme leaves
1 tablespoon lemon juice

**1** Drop beans into medium saucepan of boiling water, return to the boil; drain. When beans are cool enough to handle, peel away grey-coloured outer shells.
**2** Heat butter in large frying pan; cook shallot and speck, stirring, until speck is browned lightly. Add beans and thyme; cook, stirring, until beans are heated through. Stir in juice.

**prep + cook time** *40 minutes* **serves** *4*
**nutritional count per serving** *7.7g total fat (3.5g saturated fat); 589kJ (141 cal); 2g carbohydrate; 13.9g protein; 4.8g fibre*

# chorizo and chickpeas in white wine

1 tablespoon olive oil
1 small brown onion (80g), sliced finely
2 cloves garlic, crushed
2 chorizo (340g), chopped coarsely
1 medium red capsicum (200g), sliced finely
400g can chickpeas, rinsed, drained
½ teaspoon smoked paprika
¼ cup (60ml) dry white wine
⅓ cup (80ml) chicken stock

**1** Heat oil in large frying pan; cook onion, garlic and chorizo, stirring, until chorizo is browned lightly.
**2** Add capsicum, chickpeas and paprika; cook, stirring, until capsicum softens. Add wine and stock; cook, stirring, until liquid is reduced by half.

**prep + cook time** *25 minutes* **serves** *6*
**nutritional count per serving** *21.1g total fat (6.8g saturated fat); 1241kJ (297 cal); 9.6g carbohydrate; 14.6g protein; 3g fibre*

# braised artichokes with crunchy almond topping

6 large globe artichokes (2.4kg)
4 bay leaves
4 cloves garlic
1 litre (4 cups) chicken stock
**crunchy almond topping**
¾ cup (50g) stale breadcrumbs
⅓ cup (25g) flaked almonds
2 tablespoons finely chopped fresh
   flat-leaf parsley
½ cup (60g) seeded green olives,
   chopped finely
¼ cup (60ml) olive oil
1 tablespoon finely grated lemon rind
2 tablespoons lemon juice

**1** Preheat oven to 200°C/180°C fan-forced.
**2** Prepare artichokes by snapping off tough outer leaves and peeling stems. Trim stems to 5cm. Cut 2cm off top of artichokes to reveal chokes. Cut artichokes in half from top to bottom, then scoop out and discard furry chokes from the centres. As you finish preparing each artichoke, place it in a large bowl of water containing the juice of about half a lemon (this stops any discolouration while you are preparing the next one).
**3** Drain artichokes. Combine artichokes, bay leaves, garlic and stock in small baking dish, ensuring artichokes are covered with stock. Bake, covered, about 45 minutes or until artichokes are tender.
**4** Meanwhile, make crunchy almond topping.
**5** Drain artichokes; discard liquid.
**6** Serve artichokes hot or at room temperature sprinkled with crunchy almond topping.
**crunchy almond topping** Combine breadcrumbs and nuts on oven tray; roast about 5 minutes, cool 5 minutes. Combine breadcrumb mixture with remaining ingredients in small bowl.

prep + cook time *1 hour 40 minutes* serves *6*
nutritional count per serving *13.1g total fat (1.9g saturated fat); 928kJ (222 cal); 13.1g carbohydrate; 11.6g protein; 3.3g fibre*

# roasted thyme potatoes with spicy sauce

500g baby new potatoes, halved

2 tablespoons olive oil

1 tablespoon finely chopped fresh thyme

**spicy sauce**

1 tablespoon olive oil

1 small brown onion (80g), chopped finely

2 cloves garlic, sliced thinly

1 fresh small red thai chilli, chopped finely

410g can crushed tomatoes

2 teaspoons caster sugar

**1** Preheat oven to 220°C/200°C fan-forced.

**2** Combine potatoes, oil and thyme in large baking dish; roast about 30 minutes or until potato is tender.

**3** Meanwhile, make spicy sauce.

**4** Serve spicy sauce with hot roasted potatoes.

**spicy sauce** Heat oil in medium saucepan; cook onion, garlic and chilli, stirring occasionally, until onion is soft. Add undrained tomatoes and sugar; bring to the boil. Reduce heat; simmer, uncovered, stirring occasionally, about 10 minutes or until sauce thickens.

**prep + cook time** *45 minutes* **serves** *8*
**nutritional count per serving** *7g total fat
(1g saturated fat); 506kJ ( 121cal);
11.5g carbohydrate; 2.1g protein; 2.2g fibre*

# rosemary potatoes with leek and chorizo

500g baby new potatoes, sliced thickly
2 chorizo (340g), cut into 1-cm thick slices
1 large leek (500g), trimmed, chopped coarsely
6 cloves garlic
1 tablespoon finely chopped fresh rosemary
2 teaspoons sweet paprika
5 bay leaves
¼ cup (60ml) olive oil

1  Preheat oven to 220°C/200°C fan-forced.
2  Combine ingredients in large baking dish. Roast, uncovered, about 30 minutes or until potatoes are browned lightly.

prep + cook time *45 minutes*  serves 8
nutritional count per serving  *19.8g total fat (5.6g saturated fat); 1120kJ (268 cal); 11g carbohydrate; 10.6g protein; 2.9g fibre*

# pickled quail eggs and beetroot

12 quail eggs
500g baby beetroot, leaves trimmed
1 litre (4 cups) cider vinegar
¾ cup (165g) caster sugar
2 bay leaves
1 tablespoon black peppercorns
2 teaspoons finely grated fresh horseradish
¼ cup lightly packed fresh dill leaves

1 Sterilise 1.25-litre (5-cup) jar and lid.

2 Add eggs to small saucepan of boiling water; simmer, uncovered, about 6 minutes. Drain, then shell eggs.

3 Trim leaves from beetroot; place unpeeled beetroot in large saucepan of boiling water. Boil, covered, about 20 minutes or until beetroot are tender. Cool beetroot 10 minutes then peel.

4 Combine vinegar, sugar, bay leaves, peppercorns and horseradish in medium saucepan; stir over heat until sugar dissolves then bring to the boil. Remove from heat, stir in dill.

5 Place eggs and beetroot in hot sterilised jar; pour in enough vinegar mixture to cover eggs and beetroot. Seal jar; cool. Refrigerate overnight or for up to 1 week.

prep + cook time *1 hour*
*(+ refrigeration)* serves *6*
nutritional count per serving *1.9g total fat (0.6g saturated fat); 736kJ (176 cal); 33.9g carbohydrate; 4g protein; 2.5g fibre*

Wear disposable gloves when handling the cooked beetroot. If you squeeze the warm beetroot, the skin should burst and peel away easily.
Quail eggs are available from speciality food stores and some poultry shops.
Fresh horseradish is available from most greengrocers.

# roasted cherry tomato and parmesan dip

250g cherry tomatoes
2 teaspoons olive oil
½ cup (120g) sour cream
½ cup (40g) finely grated parmesan cheese
2 tablespoons finely chopped fresh basil
½ teaspoon dried chilli flakes
1 stick sourdough bread (200g), sliced thinly
2 cloves garlic, halved

**1** Preheat oven to 220°C/200°C fan-forced.
**2** Combine tomatoes and oil on oven tray. Roast, uncovered, about 15 minutes or until tomato skins split. Cool 10 minutes.
**3** Combine tomatoes, sour cream, cheese, basil and chilli in medium bowl.
**4** Toast bread both sides. Rub garlic onto toasts; serve with tomato and parmesan dip.

**prep + cook time** *35 minutes* **serves** *6*
**nutritional count per serving** *12.6g total fat (6.9g saturated fat); 932kJ (223 cal); 20g carbohydrate; 6.4g protein; 2.4g fibre*

# smoked eggplant and capsicum jam

1 large eggplant (500g), chopped finely
1 medium red capsicum (200g), chopped finely
1 medium red onion (170g), chopped finely
¼ cup (60ml) olive oil
1 tablespoon fresh thyme leaves
1 tablespoon smoked paprika
¼ teaspoon cayenne pepper
¼ cup (60ml) lemon juice
½ cup (125ml) water

**1** Preheat oven to 220°C/200°C fan-forced.
**2** Combine eggplant, capsicum, onion and oil on baking-paper-lined oven tray; roast, uncovered, about 30 minutes or until vegetables are browned lightly.
**3** Combine roasted vegetables, thyme, paprika, pepper, juice and the water in medium saucepan. Bring to the boil; reduce heat, simmer, uncovered, about 10 minutes or until jam is thickened.
**4** Serve jam, warm or at room temperature, with char-grilled pitta bread.

**prep + cook time** *1 hour* **serves** *8*
**nutritional count per serving** *7.1g total fat (1g saturated fat); 364kJ (87 cal); 3.8g carbohydrate; 1.4g protein; 2g fibre*

**Smoked eggplant and capsicum jam can be tossed through pasta, spread on pizza bases, or served as side dish to chicken, lamb or fish.**

# antipasto

## carpaccio

### salmon carpaccio

Tightly wrap 400g piece sashimi salmon in plastic wrap; freeze 1 hour. Unwrap salmon; slice thinly. Arrange salmon on serving platter; drizzle with 2 tablespoons white wine vinegar. Refrigerate 1 hour. Slice 2 baby fennel bulbs thinly. Reserve 2 teaspoons finely chopped fennel fronds. Combine fennel, fronds, 2 teaspoons finely grated orange rind, ¼ cup orange juice, 1 tablespoon olive oil and 1 teaspoon finely chopped fresh thyme in medium bowl. Drain excess vinegar from salmon; serve topped with fennel mixture.

---

**prep time** *30 minutes*
*(+ freezing and refrigeration)*
**serves** *8*
**nutritional count per serving**
*5.9g total fat (1.1g saturated fat);*
*414kJ (99 cal); 1.3g carbohydrate;*
*10g protein; 0.6g fibre*

### zucchini carpaccio

Using vegetable peeler, slice 3 large zucchinis lengthways into ribbons. Combine zucchini in medium bowl with 2 tablespoons olive oil, ¼ cup white wine vinegar, 2 teaspoons caster sugar, 2 tablespoons finely chopped fresh chives and 1 seeded, finely chopped medium egg tomato. Cover; refrigerate 30 minutes. Serve zucchini carpaccio sprinkled with 2 tablespoons roasted slivered almonds.

---

**prep time** *20 minutes*
*(+ refrigeration)* **serves** *8*
**nutritional count per serving**
*6g total fat (0.7g saturated fat);*
*464kJ (111 cal); 12.5g carbohydrate;*
*1.3g protein; 1.3g fibre*

### beef carpaccio

Tightly wrap 400g piece beef eye fillet in plastic wrap; freeze 1 hour or until firm. Unwrap beef; slice as thinly as possible. Arrange slices on platter. Combine 2 tablespoons olive oil, 2 teaspoons finely grated lemon rind, 2 tablespoons lemon juice, 1 crushed clove garlic, ⅓ cup finely chopped fresh flat-leaf parsley, 2 tablespoons finely chopped fresh oregano and ⅓ cup finely chopped baby rocket leaves in small bowl. Serve beef sprinkled with herb mixture and ⅓ cup flaked parmesan cheese.

prep time *30 minutes (+ freezing)* serves *8*
nutritional count per serving *7.8g total fat (2.3g saturated fat); 506kJ (121 cal); 0.3g carbohydrate; 12.3g protein; 0.3g fibre*

### kingfish carpaccio

Tightly wrap 400g piece sashimi kingfish in plastic wrap; freeze 1 hour or until firm. Unwrap fish; slice as thinly as possible. Arrange slices on platter; drizzle fish with ¼ cup lemon juice. Cover; refrigerate 1 hour. Combine 2 tablespoons olive oil, 1 small red onion, sliced thinly, 1 cup loosely packed fresh flat-leaf parsley leaves and 2 tablespoons rinsed, drained baby capers in medium bowl. Drain juice from fish; serve with onion mixture.

prep time *30 minutes (+ freezing and refrigeration)* serves *8*
nutritional count per serving *5.7g total fat (1g saturated fat); 410kJ (98 cal); 0.9g carbohydrate; 10.5g protein; 0.5g fibre*

**Use whatever firm white sashimi-type fish you like.**

### tuna carpaccio

Tightly wrap 400g piece sashimi tuna in plastic wrap; freeze 1 hour. Unwrap tuna; slice as thinly as possible. Arrange slices on platter; drizzle tuna with ¼ cup lime juice. Cover; refrigerate 1 hour. Combine 2 tablespoons olive oil, 1 finely chopped fresh long red chilli, ¼ cup finely shredded fresh basil and 2 tablespoons coarsely chopped roasted pistachios in medium bowl. Drain juice from tuna; serve tuna with basil mixture.

prep time *30 minutes (+ freezing and refrigeration)* serves *8*
nutritional count per serving *8.3g total fat (1.9g saturated fat); 535kJ (128 cal); 0.4g carbohydrate; 13g protein; 0.2g fibre*

## bites & spreads

### goats cheese and chive pastries

Preheat oven to 200°C/180°C fan-forced. Combine 240g soft goats cheese, ¼ cup finely chopped fresh chives, ¼ cup finely chopped roasted slivered almonds and ¼ cup finely chopped seeded prunes in small bowl. Spray one of 16 fillo sheets with cooking-oil spray. Top with another pastry sheet. Repeat to make four stacks. Cut each stack into four to make 16 rectangles. Place level tablespoons of cheese mixture along short sides of each rectangle. Roll pastry once over filling; fold in both sides then roll up to form cigars. Place pastries on lined oven tray; bake about 15 minutes.

**prep + cook time** *1 hour* **makes** *16*
**nutritional count per pastry**
*3.6g total fat (1.7g saturated fat);*
*351kJ (84 cal); 8.8g carbohydrate;*
*3.7g protein; 0.7g fibre*

### blue cheese toasts with pear and watercress

Preheat grill. Cut 1 small french bread stick into 1cm slices. Brush bread both sides with combined 40g melted butter and 1 clove crushed garlic; place bread, in single layer, on oven tray. Toast bread both sides. Thinly slice 1 medium pear. Spread toasts with 200g soft blue cheese; top with pear slices and 1 cup trimmed watercress.

**prep + cook time** *30 minutes*
**makes** *20*
**nutritional count per piece**
*5.2g total fat (3.2g saturated fat);*
*334kJ (80 cal); 5.2g carbohydrate;*
*2.8g protein; 0.7g fibre*

## fig and quince paste

Peel, core and quarter 1kg quinces; combine in large saucepan with 1 cup chopped dried figs, 1 cinnamon stick and enough water to cover, bring to the boil. Simmer, covered, about 1 hour or until most liquid is absorbed. Discard cinnamon; process mixture until pulpy. Measure mixture into same pan. Add 1 cup caster sugar to every 1 cup pulp; stir in ¼ cup lemon juice, stir until sugar dissolves. Cook, over very low heat, about 2 hours or until mixture leaves side of pan. Pour into oiled and lined deep 20cm-round cake pan. Stand at room temperature overnight until set. Serve as part of a cheese platter.

**prep + cook time** *3½ hours (+ standing)* **makes** *4 cups*
**nutritional count per teaspoon**
*0g total fat (0g saturated fat); 79kJ (19 cal); 4.5g carbohydrate; 0.1g protein; 0.4g fibre*

## blue cheese and caramelised onion dip

Melt 20g butter in medium saucepan; cook 1 coarsely chopped large brown onion, stirring, until onion softens. Add 2 tablespoons brown sugar and 2 tablespoons white wine vinegar; cook, stirring, over low heat, about 10 minutes or until onion is caramelised. Stir in 100g crumbled blue cheese and ¾ cup crème fraîche until smooth. Cool. Cover; refrigerate until cold. Stir in ¼ cup finely chopped fresh flat-leaf parsley.

**prep + cook time** *30 minutes* **makes** *1½ cups*
**nutritional count per teaspoon**
*1.7g total fat (1.1g saturated fat); 84kJ (20 cal); 0.7g carbohydrate; 0.4g protein; 0.1g fibre*

## baked brie

Preheat oven to 200°C/180°C fan-forced. Grease 1 cup ovenproof dish (10cm diameter, 4cm deep.) Place whole 200g brie in dish. Make six small slits into cheese. Cut 1 sprig fresh thyme into six pieces; push thyme into slits. Pour 2 tablespoons dry red wine over cheese; cover dish, place on oven tray. Bake about 20 minutes. Stand, covered, 5 minutes. Sprinkle with 1 teaspoon finely grated lemon rind and 1 finely chopped fresh thyme sprig to serve.

**prep + cook time** *40 minutes* **serves** *8*
**nutritional count per serving**
*7.3g total fat (4.7g saturated fat); 368kJ (88 cal); 0g carbohydrate; 4.8g protein; 0g fibre*

# roasted capsicum and walnut dip

2 medium red capsicums (400g)
250g cream cheese
½ cup (60g) finely chopped roasted walnuts

**1** Preheat oven to 220°C/200°C fan-forced.
**2** Quarter capsicums; discard seeds and membranes. Roast, skin-side up, until skin blisters and blackens. Cover capsicum with plastic or paper for 5 minutes; peel away skin, then chop coarsely.
**3** Blend or process capsicum and cream cheese until smooth; stir in nuts.

**prep + cook time** *40 minutes* **makes** *2 cups*
**nutritional count per teaspoon** *1.3g total fat (0.6g saturated fat); 59kJ (14 cal); 0.2g carbohydrate; 0.4g protein; 0.1g fibre*

**Serve with garlic pizza wedges, see page 53.**

# chunky olive and herb dip

½ cup (80g) finely chopped seeded green olives
½ cup finely chopped fresh flat-leaf parsley
½ cup finely chopped fresh mint
¼ cup finely chopped fresh dill
6 drained anchovy fillets, chopped finely
2 teaspoons finely grated lemon rind
¼ cup (60ml) lemon juice
½ cup (125ml) olive oil

**1** Combine ingredients in medium bowl.

**prep time** *20 minutes*  **makes** *1½ cups*
**nutritional count per teaspoon**  *1.6g total fat*
*(0.2g saturated fat); 67kJ (16 cal);*
*0.3g carbohydrate; 0.1g protein; 0.1g fibre*

**Serve with garlic pizza wedges, see page 53.**

47

# roasted fennel dip

4 baby fennel bulbs with fronds (520g)
2 cloves garlic, unpeeled
1 tablespoon olive oil
1 cup (240g) sour cream

**1** Preheat oven to 200°C/180°C fan-forced.
**2** Halve fennel lengthways; remove and discard cores. Reserve 2 teaspoons coarsely chopped fennel fronds.
**3** Combine fennel, garlic and oil in small baking dish; roast, uncovered, about 30 minutes or until fennel is tender. Cool.
**4** Peel garlic; blend or process fennel, garlic and sour cream until smooth. Serve dip sprinkled with reserved fennel fronds.

**prep + cook time** *45 minutes* **makes 1½ cups**
**nutritional count per teaspoon** *1.6g total fat (0.9g saturated fat); 67kJ (16 cal); 0.2g carbohydrate; 0.1g protein; 0.1g fibre*

**Serve with garlic pizza wedges, see page 53.**

# white bean dip

1 tablespoon olive oil
1 medium leek (350g), sliced thinly
400g can white beans, rinsed, drained
300ml cream
1 teaspoon finely grated lemon rind
1 tablespoon lemon juice
2 tablespoons finely chopped fresh
   flat-leaf parsley

**1**  Heat oil in small frying pan; cook leek, stirring, about 10 minutes or until leek softens. Cool.
**2**  Blend or process leek, beans, cream, rind and juice until smooth. Stir in parsley.

**prep + cook time** *25 minutes*  **makes** *2½ cups*
**nutritional count per teaspoon**  *1.2g total fat (0.7g saturated fat); 59kJ (14 cal); 0.4g carbohydrate; 0.2g protein; 0.2g fibre*

**Serve dip with crusty bread, if you like. We used cannellini beans in this recipe but use any white bean you like.**

# giardiniera

2 medium red capsicums (400g)

1 litre (4 cups) white vinegar

2 cups (500ml) water

6 black peppercorns

1 bay leaf

1 tablespoon sea salt flakes

1 small eggplant (230g), quartered lengthways, cut into 1cm slices

½ small cauliflower (200g), cut into florets

2 medium carrots (240g), sliced thinly diagonally

2 stalks celery (300g), trimmed, sliced thickly diagonally

2 tablespoons finely chopped fresh flat-leaf parsley

2 teaspoons finely chopped fresh thyme

2 cups (500ml) olive oil

2 cloves garlic, sliced thinly

**1** Preheat oven to 200°C/180°C fan-forced. Sterilise 1.5-litre (6-cup) jar and lid.

**2** Quarter capsicums; discard seeds and membranes. Roast capsicum, skin-side up, until skin blisters and blackens. Cover capsicum with plastic or paper for 5 minutes; peel away skin then slice thickly.

**3** Meanwhile, combine vinegar, the water, peppercorns, bay leaf and half the salt in large saucepan; heat without boiling. Add eggplant, cauliflower, carrot and celery; bring to the boil. Reduce heat; simmer, uncovered, about 5 minutes or until vegetables are tender. Drain vegetables; discard liquid.

**4** Combine hot vegetables, capsicum, herbs and remaining salt in large heatproof bowl. Spoon vegetable mixture into sterilised jar.

**5** Heat oil and garlic in small saucepan, strain into large heatproof jug; discard garlic. Carefully pour hot oil over vegetables in jar to completely cover vegetables, leaving a 1cm space between vegetables and top of jar. Seal while hot.

**prep + cook time** *1 hour* **makes** *6 cups*
**nutritional count per ¼ cup** *19.1g total fat (2.7g saturated fat); 748kJ (179 cal); 1.6g carbohydrate; 0.7g protein; 1g fibre*

**Derived from an Italian word meaning 'garden', giardiniera is an Italian dish of pickled vegetables, often served as part of an antipasto platter. Store in the refrigerator for up to three months. Serve with crusty bread or as part of an antipasto platter with cheeses and deli meats.**

# stuffed baby capsicums

24 vine sweet minicap baby capsicums (350g)
250g ricotta cheese
2 tablespoons finely grated parmesan cheese
2 tablespoons coarsely chopped
   roasted pine nuts
4 slices hot salami (40g), chopped finely
2 tablespoons finely chopped fresh oregano

**1** Preheat oven to 200°C/180°C fan-forced.
**2** Carefully cut tops from capsicums; reserve tops. Scoop out and discard seeds and membranes.
**3** Combine remaining ingredients in small bowl. Place mixture in medium piping bag fitted with 1cm plain tube. Pipe filling into capsicums; replace tops. Place capsicums, in single layer, in oiled medium shallow baking dish.
**4** Roast capsicums about 20 minutes or until tender.

**prep + cook time** *1 hour* **makes** *24*
**nutritional count per capsicum** *2.6g total fat (1g saturated fat); 138kJ (33 cal); 0.5g carbohydrate; 1.9g protein; 0.2g fibre*

You will need about two packets of vine sweet minicaps for this recipe. Stuffed baby capsicums can be served hot or cold.
We used sopressa siciliana salami in this recipe.

# garlic pizza wedges

1 cup (250ml) warm water
1 teaspoon caster sugar
7g sachet dried yeast
2½ cups (375g) plain flour
1 teaspoon salt
1 tablespoon olive oil
2 cloves garlic, crushed
2 tablespoons finely grated parmesan cheese

**1** Combine the water, sugar and yeast in small jug. Stand in warm place about 10 minutes or until frothy.
**2** Sift flour and salt into large bowl. Add yeast mixture; mix to a soft dough. Knead dough on floured surface about 10 minutes or until smooth and elastic. Place dough in oiled large bowl; cover. Stand in warm place about 1 hour or until dough is doubled in size.
**3** Preheat oven to 220°C/200°C fan-forced. Grease two oven or pizza trays.
**4** Divide dough in half. Roll each portion into a 30cm round; place on trays.
**5** Brush pizza bases with combined oil and garlic; sprinkle with cheese.
**6** Bake pizzas about 20 minutes or until browned and crisp. Cut each pizza into 16 wedges.

**prep + cook time** *1 hour (+ standing)* **makes** *32* **nutritional count per wedge** *0.9g total fat (0.2g saturated fat); 209kJ (50 cal); 8.6g carbohydrate; 1.5g protein; 0.5g fibre*

**This recipe is a good accompaniment for the dips in this book.**

# eggplant fritters

2 large eggplants (1kg)
1 cup (100g) coarsely grated mozzarella cheese
½ cup coarsely chopped fresh flat-leaf parsley
2 cloves garlic, crushed
½ cup (50g) packaged breadcrumbs
¼ cup (35g) plain flour
2 eggs
vegetable oil, for shallow-frying

**1** Preheat oven to 220°C/200°C fan-forced.
**2** Remove and discard stem ends from eggplants; prick eggplants all over with fork. Place on oiled oven tray; roast, uncovered, about 30 minutes or until soft. Cool. Peel eggplants; chop flesh finely.
**3** Combine eggplant, cheese, parsley, garlic, breadcrumbs, flour and eggs in large bowl. Using wetted hands, shape level tablespoons of mixture into oval patties.
**4** Heat oil in large frying pan; cook fritters, in batches, until browned both sides. Drain on absorbent paper. Serve with lemon wedges, if you like.

**prep + cook time** *1 hour* **makes** *36*
**nutritional count per fritter** *5.3g total fat (1g saturated fat); 272kJ (65 cal); 2.4g carbohydrate; 1.7g protein; 0.8g fibre*

**Serve fritters warm or cold.**

# pea and pancetta frittatas

1 teaspoon olive oil
4 slices pancetta (60g), chopped finely
1 clove garlic, crushed
6 eggs
⅔ cup (160ml) cream
½ cup (60g) frozen peas
⅓ cup (25g) finely grated parmesan cheese
1 tablespoon finely chopped fresh mint
1 teaspoon finely grated lemon rind
2 tablespoons crème fraîche
36 small fresh mint leaves

1  Preheat oven to 200°C/180°C fan-forced. Grease three 12-hole (1-tablespoon/20ml) mini muffin pans.
2  Heat oil in small frying pan; cook pancetta and garlic, stirring, until pancetta is crisp. Cool.
3  Whisk eggs and cream in large jug; stir in pancetta mixture, peas, cheese, mint and rind. Pour egg mixture into pan holes.
4  Bake frittatas about 12 minutes or until set. Stand in pan 5 minutes before serving topped with crème fraîche and mint leaves.

prep + cook time *30 minutes*  makes *36*
nutritional count per frittata  *3.8g total fat (2.1g saturated fat); 178kJ (43 cal); 0.4g carbohydrate; 1.9g protein; 0.1g fibre*

# roasted vegetable and mascarpone terrine

1 medium red capsicum (200g)

1 medium zucchini (120g), sliced thinly
   lengthways

2 baby eggplants (120g), sliced thinly
   lengthways

12 slices prosciutto (180g)

250g mascarpone cheese

2 eggs

¼ cup finely chopped fresh basil

**1** Preheat oven to 200°C/180°C fan-forced.

**2** Quarter capsicums; discard seeds and membranes. Roast, skin-side up, until skin blisters and blackens. Cover capsicum with plastic or paper for 5 minutes; peel away skin, then chop capsicum finely.

**3** Meanwhile, cook zucchini and eggplant, in batches, on heated oiled grill plate until tender; cool. Chop vegetables finely.

**4** Reduce oven temperature to 180°C/160°C fan-forced. Grease 8cm x 26cm bar pan.

**5** Line base and sides of pan with prosciutto, leaving 7cm overhang on sides of pan.

**6** Combine cheese and eggs in medium bowl; stir in vegetables and basil. Carefully spread mixture into pan; fold prosciutto over to cover mixture. Cover pan tightly with foil; place on oven tray.

**7** Roast terrine 30 minutes. Uncover, roast about 30 minutes or until terrine is firm. Cool. Refrigerate terrine 3 hours before cutting into 16 slices.

**prep + cook time** *1 hour 30 minutes (+ refrigeration)* **makes** *16 slices*
**nutritional count per slice** *14.9g total fat (9.4g saturated fat); 702kJ (168 cal); 1.9g carbohydrate; 6.7g protein; 0.7g fibre*

# cheese and spinach polenta

1 litre (4 cups) milk
1 cup (170g) polenta
½ cup (50g) coarsely grated mozzarella cheese
¼ cup (20g) finely grated parmesan cheese
250g finely chopped thawed, drained
    frozen spinach
250g vine-ripened cherry truss tomatoes, halved
1 tablespoon balsamic vinegar
1 tablespoon olive oil

**1** Grease 20cm x 30cm lamington pan.
**2** Bring milk to the boil in medium saucepan; gradually stir in polenta. Cook, stirring, about 10 minutes or until polenta thickens. Stir in cheeses and spinach. Spread polenta mixture into pan, cover; refrigerate 2 hours or overnight or until firm.
**3** Preheat oven to 200°C/180°C fan-forced.
**4** Turn polenta onto board; cut into 30 squares. Place polenta onto baking-paper-lined oven tray. Bake about 20 minutes or until browned lightly.
**5** Meanwhile, combine tomato, vinegar and oil in small baking dish. Roast, alongside polenta, about 15 minutes or until tomato softens slightly.
**6** Serve polenta squares topped with tomato halves; drizzle with tomato pan juices.

**prep + cook time** *45 minutes*
*(+ refrigeration)* **makes** *30*
**nutritional count per piece** *2.6g total fat*
*(1.3g saturated fat); 242kJ (58 cal);*
*5.7g carbohydrate; 2.5g protein; 0.5g fibre*

# fried bocconcini with roasted capsicum sauce

1 medium red capsicum (200g)
2 medium egg tomatoes (150g), halved
2 cloves garlic, unpeeled
2 teaspoons olive oil
2 tablespoons plain flour
1 egg, beaten lightly
½ cup (50g) packaged breadcrumbs
¼ cup (20g) finely grated parmesan cheese
2 tablespoons finely chopped fresh
    flat-leaf parsley
2 teaspoons finely grated lemon rind
16 cherry bocconcini cheese (240g)
vegetable oil, for deep-frying

**1**  Preheat oven to 220°C/200°C fan-forced.
**2**  Quarter capsicum; remove seeds and membranes. Combine capsicum, tomato, garlic and oil in small baking dish; roast, uncovered, about 20 minutes or until vegetables soften.
**3**  Peel garlic; blend or process garlic and vegetable mixture until smooth.
**4**  Place flour and egg in separate small shallow bowls. Combine breadcrumbs, parmesan, parsley and rind in another small shallow bowl.
**5**  Coat bocconcini in flour; shake off excess. Dip in egg, then in breadcrumb mixture.
**6**  Meanwhile heat oil in wok; deep-fry bocconcini, in batches, until golden. Drain on wire rack over tray.
**7**  Serve bocconcini with roasted capsicum sauce.

**prep + cook time** *1 hour*  **makes** *16*
**nutritional count per cheese ball**  *4.5g total fat*
*(2.1g saturated fat); 309kJ (74 cal);*
*3.8g carbohydrate; 4.3g protein; 0.5g fibre*

# ricotta-stuffed prosciutto and melon

½ medium rockmelon (850g)
5 slices prosciutto (75g)
150g ricotta cheese
1 tablespoon finely chopped fresh chives
2 tablespoons finely chopped roasted walnuts

**1** Peel rockmelon; cut lengthways into 10 slices. Cut each slice in half crossways.
**2** Cut prosciutto in half lengthways; cut each slice in half crossways.
**3** Combine remaining ingredients in small bowl.
**4** Spread cheese mixture over one side of each prosciutto; wrap prosciutto firmly around melon.

**prep time** *20 minutes* **makes** *20*
**nutritional count per piece** *1.8g total fat (0.7g saturated fat); 121kJ (29 cal); 1.5g carbohydrate; 1.8g protein; 0.4g fibre*

**You could use halved fresh figs instead of the rockmelon, if you like.**

# smoked trout dip

1 medium potato (200g), chopped coarsely
¼ cup (60ml) warm milk
150g piece smoked trout, flaked
1 clove garlic, crushed
2 tablespoons olive oil
2 green onions, chopped finely

1  Boil, steam or microwave potato until tender; drain. Push potato through fine sieve into small bowl; stir in milk.
2  Combine trout, garlic, oil and onion in medium bowl; fold in potato mixture.
3  Serve dip with poppy seed crackers, if you like.

prep + cook time *30 minutes* makes *1½ cups*
nutritional count per teaspoon  *0.7g total fat (0.1g saturated fat); 46kJ (11 cal); 0.4g carbohydrate; 0.7g protein; 0.1g fibre*

# fried cauliflower

1 small cauliflower (1kg), cut into florets
3 eggs
½ cup (125ml) milk
½ cup (75g) self-raising flour
¼ cup (20g) finely grated parmesan cheese
2 tablespoons finely chopped fresh
    flat-leaf parsley
vegetable oil, for deep-frying

1   Boil, steam or microwave cauliflower until tender; drain. Cool.
2   Whisk eggs, milk, flour, cheese and parsley in medium shallow bowl until smooth.
3   Heat oil in wok. Dip cauliflower into batter; drain off excess. Deep-fry cauliflower, in batches, until browned lightly. Drain on absorbent paper.
4   Serve cauliflower with lemon wedges, if you like.

**prep + cook time** *40 minutes* **serves 16**
**nutritional count per serving  4.6g total fat**
**(1.1g saturated fat); 326kJ (78 cal);**
**4.9g carbohydrate; 3.7g protein; 1.2g fibre**

# marinated mushrooms

1 litre (4 cups) white vinegar
1 cup (250ml) dry white wine
1 tablespoon sea salt flakes
800g button mushrooms, halved
2 cloves garlic, sliced thinly
½ teaspoon dried chilli flakes
1 tablespoon coarsely chopped fresh rosemary
1 tablespoon finely chopped fresh
    flat-leaf parsley
3 x 5cm strips lemon rind
1 bay leaf
2 cups (500ml) olive oil

**1** Sterilise 1-litre (4-cup) jar and lid.
**2** Combine vinegar, wine and half the salt in medium saucepan; heat without boiling. Add mushrooms; simmer, uncovered, about 5 minutes or until tender. Drain mushrooms; discard liquid.
**3** Combine hot mushrooms, garlic, chilli, herbs, rind, bay leaf and remaining salt in large heatproof bowl. Spoon mushroom mixture into hot sterilised jar.
**4** Heat oil in small saucepan; carefully pour over mushrooms in jar to completely cover mushrooms, leaving a 1cm space between mushrooms and top of jar. Seal while hot.

**prep + cook time** *40 minutes* **makes** *4 cups*
**nutritional count per ¼ cup** *28.6g total fat (4g saturated fat); 1145kJ (274 cal); 0.2g carbohydrate; 1.9g protein; 1.3g fibre*

Store marinated mushrooms in refrigerator for up to three months. Serve mushrooms with crusty bread or as part of an antipasto platter with cheeses and deli meats.

# veal braciole

⅔ cup (45g) stale breadcrumbs
1 tablespoon rinsed drained baby capers,
    chopped finely
2 cloves garlic, crushed
5 veal schnitzels (500g) (*see note, below*)
1 medium lemon (140g), quartered, sliced thickly
20 fresh bay leaves
1 tablespoon olive oil

**1** Combine breadcrumbs, capers and garlic in small bowl.
**2** Using meat mallet, gently pound veal, one piece at a time, between sheets of plastic wrap until 5mm thick; cut each piece in half crossways.
**3** Press 1 level tablespoon of crumb mixture over one side of each piece of veal. Roll veal up tightly; cut each roll in half.
**4** Thread lemon slices, veal rolls and bay leaves onto 20 small bamboo skewers or strong toothpicks. Brush skewers all over with oil; cook on heated oiled grill plate (or grill or barbecue) until veal is cooked through.

**prep + cook time** *40 minutes* **makes** *20*
**nutritional count per piece** *1.4g total fat*
*(0.2g saturated fat); 184kJ (44 cal);*
*1.7g carbohydrate; 5.9g protein; 0.3g fibre*

**We used plain uncrumbed schnitzel, sometimes called escalopes, in this recipe.**
**You need 20 small bamboo skewers or strong toothpicks for this recipe. Soak skewers in cold water at least an hour before using to prevent them scorching during cooking.**

# arancini

2 cups (500ml) chicken stock
½ cup (125ml) dry white wine
40g butter
1 small brown onion (80g), chopped finely
1 clove garlic, crushed
1 cup (200g) arborio rice
⅓ cup (25g) finely grated parmesan cheese
⅓ cup (35g) coarsely grated mozzarella cheese
24 fetta-stuffed green olives (240g)
⅓ cup (35g) packaged breadcrumbs
vegetable oil, for deep-frying

**1** Combine stock and wine in medium saucepan; bring to the boil. Reduce heat; simmer, covered.
**2** Meanwhile, melt butter in medium saucepan; cook onion and garlic, stirring, until onion softens. Add rice; stir over medium heat until rice is coated in butter mixture. Stir in ½ cup of the simmering stock mixture; cook, stirring, over low heat until liquid is absorbed. Continue adding mixture, in ½ cup batches, stirring, until liquid is absorbed after each addition. Total cooking time should be about 35 minutes or until rice is tender. Stir in cheeses, cover; cool 30 minutes.
**3** Roll rounded tablespoons of risotto mixture into balls; press an olive into centre of each ball, roll to enclose. Coat risotto balls in breadcrumbs.
**4** Heat oil in wok; deep-fry risotto balls, in batches, until browned lightly. Drain on absorbent paper.

**prep + cook time** *1 hour 30 minutes* *(+ cooling)* **makes** *24*
**nutritional count per ball** *5.7g total fat (1.8g saturated fat); 401kJ (96 cal); 8.1g carbohydrate; 1.9g protein; 1g fibre*

# risotto-filled zucchini flowers

2 cups (500ml) chicken stock
½ cup (125ml) dry white wine
pinch saffron
40g butter
1 small brown onion (80g), chopped finely
1 clove garlic, crushed
1 cup (200g) arborio rice
⅓ cup (25g) finely grated parmesan cheese
1 teaspoon finely grated lemon rind
2 tablespoons finely chopped fresh
    flat-leaf parsley
28 zucchini flowers with stem attached (420g)
cooking-oil spray

**1** Combine stock, wine and saffron in medium saucepan; bring to the boil. Reduce heat; simmer, covered.

**2** Meanwhile, melt butter in medium saucepan; cook onion and garlic, stirring, until onion softens. Add rice; stir over medium heat until rice is coated in butter mixture. Stir in ½ cup of the simmering stock mixture; cook, stirring, over low heat until liquid is absorbed. Continue adding stock mixture, in ½ cup batches, stirring, until liquid is absorbed after each addition. Total cooking time should be about 35 minutes or until rice is tender. Stir in cheese, rind and parsley, cover; cool 30 minutes.

**3** Preheat oven to 200°C/180°C fan-forced. Grease two oven trays.

**4** Discard stamens from zucchini flowers; fill flowers with 1 level tablespoon of risotto mixture, twist petal tops to enclose filling.

**5** Place zucchini flowers on trays; spray all over with cooking-oil spray. Roast, uncovered, about 15 minutes or until zucchini stems are tender.

**prep + cook time** *1 hour 30 minutes*
*(+ cooking)* **makes** *28*
**nutritional count per flower** *1.8g total fat*
*(1g saturated fat); 209kJ (50 cal);*
*6.2g carbohydrate; 1.3g protein; 0.4g fibre*

**If you don't want to make 28 zucchini flowers –
just eat the delicious risotto as it is.**

# tomato tarts

4 medium vine-ripened tomatoes (600g),
    peeled, quartered, seeded
1 tablespoon brown sugar
1 tablespoon balsamic vinegar
½ sheet ready-rolled puff pastry
16 sprigs fresh chervil

**1** Preheat oven 220°C/200°C fan-forced.
**2** Combine tomato, sugar and vinegar in small baking dish; roast, uncovered, about 20 minutes or until tomato is soft.
**3** Meanwhile, cut pastry sheet in half lengthways, cut each half into 4 squares; cut each square into triangles (you will have 16). Place pastry triangles on oiled oven tray; top with another oiled oven tray (the second tray stops the pastry from puffing up). Bake pastry, alongside tomato, about 10 minutes or until crisp.
**4** Place a tomato piece on each pastry triangle. Serve topped with chervil.

**prep + cook time** *40 minutes* **makes** *16*
**nutritional count per tart** *1.2g total fat (0.6g saturated fat); 117kJ (28 cal); 3.4g carbohydrate; 0.7g protein; 0.5g fibre*

# sweet and sour beetroot

2 large beetroot (400g), peeled,
   grated coarsely
3 green onions, sliced thinly
1 tablespoon finely chopped fresh dill
2 tablespoons red wine vinegar
1 tablespoon olive oil
1 teaspoon wholegrain mustard
2 teaspoons caster sugar
1 witlof (125g), leaves separated (*see note*)

1  Combine beetroot, onion, dill, vinegar, oil,
mustard and sugar in medium bowl.
2  Serve beetroot mixture with witlof leaves.

**prep time** *15 minutes* **makes** *24*
**nutritional count per piece** *0.8g total fat*
*(0.1g saturated fat); 71kJ (17 cal);*
*1.7g carbohydrate; 0.4g protein; 0.6g fibre*

**You need 24 witlof leaves for this recipe.**

# meatballs napolitana

500g beef mince
1 egg
½ cup (50g) packaged breadcrumbs
¼ cup (20g) finely grated parmesan cheese
¼ cup finely chopped fresh flat-leaf parsley
2 tablespoons olive oil
1 small brown onion (80g), chopped finely
1 clove garlic, crushed
700g bottled tomato pasta sauce
½ cup (60g) frozen peas
¼ cup coarsely chopped fresh basil

**1** Combine mince, egg, breadcrumbs, cheese and parsley in medium bowl. Using wetted hands, roll level tablespoons of mince mixture into balls.
**2** Heat half the oil in large frying pan; cook meatballs, in batches, until browned and cooked through.
**3** Heat remaining oil in same pan; cook onion and garlic, stirring, until onion softens. Add sauce; bring to the boil. Add meatballs, reduce heat; simmer, uncovered, about 10 minutes or until sauce thickens slightly. Add peas and basil; simmer, uncovered, until peas are tender.
**4** Serve meatballs and sauce with crusty bread, if you like.

**prep + cook time** *1 hour* **makes** *26*
**nutritional count per meatball** *3.9g total fat (1.2g saturated fat); 305kJ (73 cal); 4.1g carbohydrate; 4.9g protein; 0.8g fibre*

# fish and caper croquettes

¾ cup (180ml) water
¾ cup (180ml) dry white wine
2 bay leaves
400g skinless boneless firm white fish fillets
40g butter
¼ cup (35g) plain flour
1 cup (250ml) milk
2 teaspoons finely grated lemon rind
2 tablespoons rinsed drained baby capers,
    chopped finely
1 clove garlic, crushed
1 tablespoon finely chopped fresh chives
¼ cup (35g) plain flour, extra
1 egg, beaten lightly
1 cup (70g) stale breadcrumbs
vegetable oil, for shallow-frying
1 medium lemon, sliced thickly

**1** Combine the water, wine and bay leaves in small saucepan; bring to the boil. Add fish, reduce heat; simmer, covered, about 5 minutes or until fish is cooked through. Drain fish; discard cooking liquid, flake fish coarsely.
**2** Meanwhile, melt butter in medium saucepan. Add flour; cook, stirring, about 2 minutes or until mixture thickens and bubbles. Gradually stir in milk; cook, stirring, until mixture boils and thickens. Remove from heat; stir in rind, capers, garlic, chives and fish. Cover; refrigerate 2 hours.
**3** Roll rounded tablespoons of fish mixture into ovals; coat in extra flour, shake off excess. Dip croquettes in egg then breadcrumbs.
**4** Heat oil in large frying pan; cook croquettes until browned all over. Drain on absorbent paper. Serve with lemon slices.

**prep + cook time** *40 minutes*
*(+ refrigeration)* **makes 16**
**nutritional count per croquette** *7.9g total fat*
*(2.6g saturated fat); 573kJ (137 cal);*
*7.2g carbohydrate; 7.2g protein; 0.6g fibre*

# mezze

## skewers

**Soak skewers in water for at least an hour prior to using to prevent them from scorching during cooking.**

### lemon, garlic and oregano lamb skewers

Cut 800g lamb fillets into 2cm pieces. Combine lamb in medium bowl with 1 tablespoon olive oil, 2 teaspoons finely grated lemon rind, 1 clove crushed garlic and 2 tablespoons finely chopped fresh oregano. Cover; refrigerate 1 hour. Stir in 1 tablespoon lemon juice. Thread lamb onto 16 small bamboo skewers or strong toothpicks; cook skewers on heated oiled grill plate (or grill or barbecue) until cooked through.

**prep + cook time** *30 minutes (+ refrigeration)* **makes 16**
**nutritional count per skewer**
*2.9g total fat (1g saturated fat); 284kJ (68 cal); 0g carbohydrate; 10.3g protein; 0g fibre*

### sumac and sesame chicken skewers

Cut 600g chicken breast fillets into 2cm cubes; thread onto 16 small bamboo skewers or strong toothpicks. Combine 1 tablespoon sumac, 1 teaspoon sesame seeds and 1 teaspoon black sesame seeds in small bowl; sprinkle sumac mixture all over skewers. Cook skewers on heated oiled grill plate (or grill or barbecue) until chicken is cooked through. Serve with lemon wedges.

**prep + cook time** *30 minutes* **makes 16**
**nutritional count per skewer**
*2.6g total fat (0.7g saturated fat); 222kJ (53 cal); 0g carbohydrate; 8.1g protein; 0g fibre*

## vegetable and haloumi skewers

Cut 180g haloumi cheese into sixteen 2cm cubes; cut 1 small red capsicum into 2cm pieces. Cut 1 large zucchini in half lengthways; cut each half into eight 2cm pieces. Thread haloumi, capsicum and zucchini onto 16 small bamboo skewers or strong toothpicks. Cook skewers on heated oiled grill plate (or grill or barbecue) until tender. Meanwhile, combine ½ cup mayonnaise, 1 tablespoon lime juice and 2 teaspoons harissa in small bowl. Serve skewers with lime and harissa mayonnaise.

**prep + cook time** *35 minutes*
**makes** *16*
**nutritional count per skewer**
*26.2g total fat (4g saturated fat); 1296kJ (310 cal); 15.6g carbohydrate; 3.4g protein; 0.7g fibre*

## lamb kebabs with yogurt and pitta bread

Combine 500g lamb mince, 1 egg, 1 finely chopped small brown onion, 2 tablespoons finely chopped fresh flat-leaf parsley, 1 crushed clove garlic, 2 teaspoons each ground cinnamon and sweet paprika and ½ teaspoon cayenne pepper in bowl. Form lamb mixture into 16 sausage shapes, thread onto 16 small bamboo skewers or strong toothpicks; flatten slightly. Cook on heated oiled grill plate (or grill or barbecue) until browned and cooked as desired. Serve kebabs with ½ cup yogurt, lemon wedges and pita bread.

**prep + cook time** *30 minutes*
**serves 4 (makes 16 skewers)**
**nutritional count per serving**
*10.8g total fat (4.8g saturated fat); 1004kJ (240 cal); 5.6g carbohydrate; 29.2g protein; 0.4g fibre*

## chermoula prawn skewers

Shell and devein 16 uncooked medium king prawns, leaving tails intact. Combine prawns with 1 tablespoon olive oil, 2 tablespoons each finely chopped fresh flat-leaf parsley, mint and coriander, 2 cloves crushed garlic, 2 teaspoons finely grated lemon rind, 1 tablespoon lemon juice, 1 teaspoon ground allspice and 1 teaspoon caraway seeds in medium bowl. Preheat grill. Thread prawns, tail-end first, onto 16 small bamboo skewers or strong toothpicks; grill prawns about 5 minutes or until changed in colour.

**prep + cook time** *30 minutes*
**makes** *16*
**nutritional count per skewer**
*1.3g total fat (0.2g saturated fat); 130kJ (31 cal); 0.1g carbohydrate; 4.7g protein; 0.1g fibre*

## pide

## basic pide dough

Combine 7g yeast, 1 teaspoon sugar, ⅔ cup warm water and 2 tablespoons warm milk in jug. Stand in warm place until frothy. Place ½ cup plain flour in bowl; whisk in yeast mixture. Cover; stand in warm place 1 hour. Stir 1½ cups plain flour and 1 teaspoon salt into yeast mixture with 1 tablespoon olive oil. Knead dough on floured surface until smooth. Place in oiled bowl, cover; stand in warm place 1 hour. Make pide. Or, preheat oven to 240°C/220°C fan-forced. Roll dough into 35cm oval; place dough on baking paper. Make indents with finger and brush over 1 tablespoon olive oil; sprinkle with 2 teaspoons black sesame seeds. Heat oven tray; lift dough onto tray on paper; bake pide about 15 minutes.

**prep + cook time** *30 minutes (+ standing)* **serves** *8*
**nutritional count per serving**
*5.6g total fat (0.8g saturated fat); 736kJ (176 cal); 26g carbohydrate; 4.4g protein; 1.6g fibre*

## egg and cheese pide

Preheat oven to 240°C/220°C fan-forced. Divide 1 quantity basic pide dough into three pieces; roll each piece to 12cm x 30cm. Brush edges of dough with a little water; fold 2cm border around edges of dough, press down firmly. Fold in corners to make oval shape. Heat oven trays in oven for 3 minutes. Quickly place pide on hot trays; bake pide 5 minutes. Remove from oven; press centre of pide down to flatten. Whisk 3 eggs with 90g coarsely grated haloumi cheese and 1 finely chopped green onion in large jug. Pour into the cavities of the pide. Bake further 10 minutes or until set. Cut each pide into eight slices; serve with lemon wedges.

**prep + cook time** *25 minutes*
**serves** *8*
**nutritional count per serving**
*9.5g total fat (2.7g saturated fat); 970kJ (232 cal); 26.3g carbohydrate; 9.3g protein; 1.6g fibre*

## lamb and tomato pide

Preheat oven to 240°C/220°C fan-forced. Heat 1 tablespoon olive oil in pan; cook 1 chopped brown onion and 1 clove crushed garlic. Add 300g lamb mince, 1 teaspoon each ground cinnamon, cumin and smoked paprika and ½ teaspoon cayenne pepper; cook until lamb is browned. Stir in 1 tablespoon chopped fresh coriander; cool. Divide 1 quantity basic dough into three; roll each piece to 12cm x 30cm. Spread filling across centre of each piece, leaving 2cm border. Brush edges with water; fold and press around dough. Fold corners to make oval shape. Heat oven trays 3 minutes, place pide on trays; bake 10 minutes. Sprinkle with 1 chopped tomato; bake 5 minutes.

**prep + cook time** *35 minutes*
**serves** *8*
**nutritional count per serving**
*10.5g total fat (2.4g saturated fat); 1087kJ (260 cal); 27.5g carbohydrate; 12.6g protein; 2.2g fibre*

## spinach and fetta pide

Preheat oven to 240°C/220°C fan-forced. Boil, steam or microwave 300g spinach until wilted. Rinse, drain then squeeze out excess water; shred spinach finely. Combine spinach, 100g crumbled fetta cheese and 90g coarsely grated haloumi cheese in medium bowl. Divide 1 quantity basic dough into three; roll each to 12cm x 30cm. Spread filling across centre of each piece, leaving 2cm border. Brush edges with water; fold and press around dough. Fold corners to make oval shape. Heat oven trays 3 minutes, place pide on trays; bake 15 minutes. Cut each pide into eight slices.

**prep + cook time** *25 minutes*
**serves** *8*
**nutritional count per serving**
*10.5g total fat (4g saturated fat); 1028kJ (246 cal); 26.5g carbohydrate; 9.9g protein; 2.6g fibre*

## pumpkin and fetta pide

Preheat oven to 240°C/220°C fan-forced. Boil, steam or microwave 200g chopped pumpkin until tender; drain, cool. Combine pumpkin, 100g chopped fetta cheese and ½ cup coarsely grated mozzarella cheese in medium bowl. Divide 1 quantity basic dough into three; roll each to 12cm x 30cm. Spread filling across centre of each piece, leaving 2cm border. Brush edges with water; fold and press around dough. Fold corners to make oval shape. Heat oven trays 3 minutes, place pide on trays; bake 15 minutes. Sprinkle pide with 1 tablespoon finely chopped fresh flat-leaf parsley. Cut each pide into eight slices.

**prep + cook time** *30 minutes*
**serves** *8*
**nutritional count per serving**
*10.2g total fat (3.9g saturated fat); 1020kJ (244 cal); 26.7g carbohydrate; 9.1g protein; 1.9g fibre*

# chicken, spinach and cheese gözleme

2 cups (300g) plain flour
½ teaspoon salt
¾ cup (180ml) warm water
2 tablespoons olive oil
1 medium brown onion (150g), chopped finely
2 cloves garlic, crushed
2 teaspoons ground cumin
1 teaspoon ground cinnamon
200g spinach, trimmed
1 cup finely shredded cooked chicken
100g fetta cheese, crumbled
2 tablespoons lemon juice

1 Combine flour and salt in medium bowl. Gradually stir in the water; mix to a soft dough. Knead dough on floured surface about 5 minutes or until smooth and elastic. Return to bowl; cover, while preparing filling.

2 Heat half the oil in medium frying pan; cook onion and garlic, stirring, until onion softens. Add spices; cook, stirring, until fragrant. Transfer mixture to medium heatproof bowl; cool.

3 Meanwhile, boil, steam or microwave spinach until wilted; rinse under cold water, drain. Squeeze out excess water; shred spinach finely. Stir spinach, chicken, cheese and juice into onion mixture.

4 Divide dough in half; roll each piece on floured surface into 25cm x 35cm rectangle. Divide spinach filling across centre of each rectangle. Fold top and bottom edges of dough over filling; tuck in ends to enclose.

5 Cook gözleme, both sides, on heated oiled grill plate (or grill or barbecue), over low heat, brushing with remaining oil until browned lightly and heated through. Stand 5 minutes before cutting each gözleme into 8 slices; serve with lemon wedges, if you like.

**prep + cook time** *1 hour 30 minutes* **makes** *16*
**nutritional count per slice** *4.6g total fat (1.5g saturated fat); 514kJ (123 cal); 14.2g carbohydrate; 5.5g protein; 1.1g fibre*

# fried fish sandwiches

2 cloves garlic, unpeeled
½ cup (140g) greek-style yogurt
¼ cup finely chopped fresh mint
8 small white fish fillets (320g), skin on
2 tablespoons plain flour
2 teaspoons smoked paprika
1 teaspoon ground cumin
1 tablespoon olive oil
1 loaf turkish bread (430g), split, toasted
1 baby cos lettuce, leaves separated
2 medium tomatoes (300g), sliced thinly
½ small red onion (50g), sliced thinly

**1** Preheat oven to 200°C/180°C fan-forced.
**2** Place garlic on oven tray; roast, uncovered, about 10 minutes or until soft. Cool; peel garlic.
**3** Blend or process garlic and yogurt until smooth; stir in mint.
**4** Coat fish in combined flour and spices; shake off excess. Heat oil in large frying pan; cook fish, both sides, until browned and crisp.
**5** Spread yogurt over one half of bread; top with lettuce, tomato, onion, fish and remaining bread. Cut into 12 slices.

**prep + cook time** *30 minutes* **makes** *12*
**nutritional count per slice** *4.2g total fat (1.1g saturated fat); 673kJ (161 cal); 19.5g carbohydrate; 10.1g protein; 1.8g fibre*

**We used sand whiting fillets in this recipe.**

# barbecued baby octopus

1kg baby octopus
⅓ cup (80ml) lemon juice
⅓ cup (80ml) olive oil
2 cloves garlic, crushed
2 teaspoons dried rigani
1 medium lemon, cut into wedges

**1** Clean octopus, remove eyes and beaks.
Combine octopus with juice, oil, garlic and rigani in
medium bowl. Cover, refrigerate 3 hours or overnight.
**2** Drain octopus; discard marinade. Cook octopus
on heated oiled barbecue (or grill or grill plate) until
tender. Serve with lemon wedges.

**prep + cook time** *25 minutes*
*(+ refrigeration)* serves 6
**nutritional count per serving** *13.4g total fat*
*(1.7g saturated fat); 982kJ (235 cal);*
*1g carbohydrate; 27.6g protein; 0.2g fibre*

**Rigani is a type of wild oregano. It has a
stronger flavour than regular oregano and is
used in many Greek dishes. You can find rigani
at specialty supermarkets and delicatessens. If
unavailable, use dried oregano.
Octopus is best cooked just before serving.**

# radish and herb salad

2 large pitta breads (160g), cut into wedges

1 medium green capsicum (200g),
  chopped finely

1 lebanese cucumber (130g), seeded,
  chopped finely

1 medium tomato (150g), chopped finely

4 red radishes (140g), grated coarsely

½ cup finely chopped fresh flat-leaf parsley

⅓ cup finely chopped fresh mint

¼ cup coarsely chopped fresh coriander

2 tablespoons olive oil

2 tablespoons lemon juice

2 cloves garlic, crushed

**1** Preheat grill.

**2** Place bread on oven trays; grill about 5 minutes or until browned both sides and crisp.

**3** Combine remaining ingredients in medium bowl. Serve salad with pitta crisps.

**prep + cook time** *25 minutes* **serves** *8*
**nutritional count per serving** *5.2g total fat (0.7g saturated fat); 468kJ (112 cal); 12.6g carbohydrate; 2.8g protein; 1.9g fibre*

# spicy tunisian tuna salad

2 teaspoons caraway seeds

½ teaspoon ground cinnamon

425g can tuna in oil

300g can chickpeas, rinsed, drained

1 small green capsicum (150g),
    cut into 1cm pieces

⅓ cup (40g) seeded black olives,
    chopped coarsely

200g red grape tomatoes, quartered

2 green onions, sliced thinly

2 teaspoons finely grated orange rind

2 tablespoons orange juice

1 tablespoon harissa

**1**  Dry-fry spices in small frying pan until fragrant; cool.

**2**  Drain tuna; reserve 2 tablespoons of the oil. Flake tuna coarsely.

**3**  Combine tuna, reserved oil, spices and remaining ingredients in large bowl. Serve with toasted turkish bread.

**prep + cook time** *25 minutes*  **serves** *8*
**nutritional count per serving**  *12g total fat (1.8g saturated fat); 782kJ (187 cal); 6.2g carbohydrate; 12.7g protein; 2.1g fibre*

# pickled octopus

1.5kg large octopus
¾ cup (180ml) extra virgin olive oil
½ cup (125ml) white wine vinegar
1 clove garlic, crushed
2 tablespoons coarsely chopped fresh
   flat-leaf parsley

**1** Clean octopus, remove eyes and beak. Place octopus in large saucepan without any liquid. Cover pan, cook over low heat about 1 hour or until octopus is tender. (The octopus will cook in its own juices but, if necessary, add a little water if the juices evaporate.) Cool octopus in pan until it is cool enough to handle. Rinse octopus under cold water, remove skin, leaving tentacles intact.
**2** Cut octopus into bite-size pieces; combine in medium bowl with remaining ingredients. Cover, refrigerate overnight. Serve sprinkled with parsley; accompany with lemon wedges, if you like.

**prep + cook time** *1 hour 10 minutes*
*(+ cooling and refrigeration)* **serves** *8*
**nutritional count per serving** *21.8g total fat*
*(2.9g saturated fat); 1333kJ (319 cal);*
*0.2g carbohydrate; 30.8g protein; 0.1g fibre*

**We used large octopus in this recipe,
but you could also use baby octopus.
Recipe can be made up to four days ahead;
store, covered, in the refrigerator.**

# blood orange and chilli glazed quail

6 quails (960g)
1 teaspoon cumin seeds
½ cup (125ml) blood orange juice
1 fresh long red chilli, chopped finely
1 clove garlic, crushed
2 tablespoons brown sugar
1 tablespoon finely chopped fresh coriander

**1** Using kitchen scissors, cut along both sides of quails' backbones; discard backbones. Halve each quail along breastbone; cut each in half again to give a total of 24 pieces.
**2** Cook quail, covered, on heated oiled grill plate (or grill or barbecue) about 20 minutes or until cooked through.
**3** Meanwhile, dry-fry seeds in small saucepan until fragrant. Add juice, chilli, garlic and sugar; stir over heat, without boiling, until sugar dissolves. Bring to the boil; boil, uncovered, about 5 minutes or until mixture is thick and syrupy.
**4** Combine hot quail, syrup and coriander in large bowl.

**prep + cook time** *35 minutes*  **serves** *8*
**nutritional count per serving**  *6.6g total fat (1.7g saturated fat); 514kJ (123 cal); 4.4g carbohydrate; 11.3g protein; 0.1g fibre*

**Quails are available from specialist food stores and most poultry shops.**

# turkish tomato salad

1 teaspoon cumin seeds
2 medium tomatoes (300g), chopped finely
1 medium red capsicum (200g), chopped finely
1 small red onion (100g), chopped finely
1 fresh long red chilli, chopped finely
¼ cup finely chopped fresh flat-leaf parsley
1 tablespoon pomegranate molasses
2 tablespoons olive oil

**1** Dry-fry seeds in small frying pan until fragrant; cool.
**2** Combine seeds with remaining ingredients in medium bowl. Serve with toasted turkish bread.

**prep + cook time** *20 minutes* **serves 8**
**nutritional count per serving** *4.6g total fat*
*(0.6g saturated fat); 234kJ (56 cal);*
*2.3g carbohydrate; 0.9g protein; 1g fibre*

# grilled haloumi

500g haloumi cheese

2 tablespoons lemon juice

1 tablespoon coarsely chopped fresh
   flat-leaf parsley

**1** Cut cheese into 1cm slices. Cook cheese on heated oiled flat plate until browned both sides. Transfer cheese to serving plate; drizzle with juice. Serve immediately, sprinkled with parsley.

**prep + cook time** *10 minutes*  **serves** *6*
**nutritional count per serving**  *14.3g total fat
(9.2g saturated fat); 861kJ (206 cal);
1.7g carbohydrate; 17.8g protein; 0g fibre*

**Haloumi is best cooked just before serving as it becomes tough and rubbery on cooling.**

# cheese pastries

1½ cups (225g) plain flour
1½ cups (225g) self-raising flour
½ teaspoon salt
¾ cup (180ml) warm water
¼ cup (60ml) olive oil
1 egg, beaten lightly
2 teaspoons sesame seeds
**filling**
1 egg, beaten lightly
100g fetta cheese, crumbled
½ cup (120g) ricotta cheese
½ cup (40g) finely grated romano cheese

**1** Preheat oven to 200°C/180°C fan-forced. Oil oven trays; line with baking paper.
**2** Process flours and salt until combined. While motor is operating, add enough of the combined water and oil so the mixture forms a ball (do not overmix). Remove dough from bowl, wrap in plastic; cover, refrigerate 30 minutes.
**3** Meanwhile, make filling.
**4** Divide dough in half. Roll each half on floured surface to 30cm x 40cm rectangle; cut 13 x 8.5cm rounds from dough. Drop rounded teaspoons of filling onto rounds; brush edges with a little water. Fold rounds in half, press edges together with a fork to seal. Place pastries on trays; brush with egg, sprinkle with seeds. Bake about 15 minutes or until browned lightly.
**filling** Combine ingredients in medium bowl.

**prep + cook time** *1 hour 15 minutes*
*(+ refrigeration)* **makes** *26*
**nutritional count per pastry** *4.7g total fat*
*(1.6g saturated fat); 456kJ (109 cal);*
*12.4g carbohydrate; 4g protein; 0.7g fibre*

**Parmesan cheese can be used instead of romano cheese. Pastries can be served warm or cold. Uncooked pastries are suitable to freeze. It is best to cut pastry into the 26 rounds from the first rolling of pastry, as the pastry is not suitable to reroll.**

# greek eggplant dip

2 large eggplants (1kg), unpeeled
1 tablespoon coarse cooking salt
¼ cup (60ml) olive oil
½ cup (140g) greek-style yogurt
1 medium white onion (150g), grated coarsely
⅓ cup coarsely chopped fresh flat-leaf parsley
2 tablespoons lemon juice
2 cloves garlic, crushed

**1** Cut eggplant into 1cm slices. Place in colander, sprinkle with salt; stand 30 minutes. Rinse eggplant under cold water; drain on absorbent paper.
**2** Preheat grill.
**3** Brush both sides of eggplant with oil; grill, in batches, until browned both sides and tender. When cool enough to handle remove skin from eggplant.
**4** Process eggplant with remaining ingredients until combined. Refrigerate 3 hours or overnight.

**prep + cook time** *45 minutes*
*(+ standing and refrigeration)* **makes 1½ cups**
**nutritional count per teaspoon** *2.3g total fat*
*(0.6g saturated fat); 125kJ (30 cal);*
*0.4g carbohydrate; 1.9g protein; 0.1g fibre*

**Serve dip with fresh crusty bread. Dip can be made three days ahead; store, covered, in the refrigerator.**

# rosewater and sesame chicken drumettes

**20 chicken drumettes (1.4kg)**
**2 tablespoons brown sugar**
**⅓ cup (80ml) rosewater**
**1 tablespoon olive oil**
**½ teaspoon ground allspice**
**2 teaspoons sesame seeds**

**1**  Using small sharp knife pierce chicken all over. Combine chicken, sugar, rosewater, oil and spice in large bowl. Cover; refrigerate 3 hours or overnight.
**2**  Preheat oven to 220°C/200°C fan-forced.
**3**  Place chicken on oiled wire rack over large baking dish; pour over any remaining marinade, sprinkle with seeds. Roast chicken, uncovered, basting with pan juices occasionally, about 30 minutes or until cooked through.

**prep + cook time** *35 minutes*
*(+ refrigeration)* **makes** *20*
**nutritional count per drumette**  *5.3g total fat*
*(1.4g saturated fat); 330kJ (79 cal);*
*1.3g carbohydrate; 6.8g protein; 0g fibre*

# spinach and fetta triangles

2 teaspoons olive oil

3 green onions, chopped finely

250g baby spinach leaves

250g fetta cheese, crumbled

2 tablespoons finely chopped fresh
    flat-leaf parsley

1 tablespoon finely chopped fresh dill

1 egg

24 sheets fillo pastry

150g ghee or butter, melted

**1** Heat oil in large frying pan, add onion; cook, stirring, until onion is softened. Add spinach; cook, stirring, until spinach is wilted. Remove from heat. When cool enough to handle, squeeze excess moisture from spinach; chop coarsely.

**2** Combine spinach mixture in medium bowl with cheese, herbs and egg.

**3** Preheat oven to 200°C/180°C fan-forced. Oil oven trays; line with baking paper.

**4** Brush 1 sheet of pastry with ghee; top with a second sheet and brush with ghee. Cut layered sheets into 4 strips lengthways. Place rounded teaspoons of spinach mixture at one end of each strip. Fold one corner of pastry diagonally over filling to form a triangle. Continue folding to end of strip, retaining triangular shape. Brush triangles with a little ghee. Repeat to make a total of 48 triangles.

**5** Place triangles on trays. Bake about 15 minutes or until browned lightly.

**prep + cook time** *1 hour 30 minutes* **makes** *48*
**nutritional count per triangle** *4.8g total fat (3g saturated fat); 280kJ (67 cal); 3.9g carbohydrate; 1.9g protein; 0.3g fibre*

**You need to buy a 375g packet of fillo pastry. To prevent pastry drying out, cover with plastic wrap or a damp tea towel until ready to use. Uncooked triangles are suitable to freeze. Ghee browns the pastry more evenly than butter.**

# beetroot and yogurt dip

500g beetroot
½ cup (140g) greek-style yogurt
1 clove garlic, crushed
2 tablespoons lemon juice
2 tablespoons coarsely chopped fresh mint

**1**  Preheat oven to 200°C/180°C fan-forced. Oil oven tray; line with baking paper.
**2**  Wash beetroot well, cut off leaves. Place unpeeled beetroot on oven tray. Roast about 1 hour or until tender. When beetroot are cool enough to handle, peel and chop coarsely; cool.
**3**  Process beetroot. Add remaining ingredients; process until smooth. Serve beetroot dip with torn pieces of heated pitta bread.

**prep + cook time** *1 hour 30 minutes*
**makes** *1⅓ cups*
**nutritional count per teaspoon**  *0.2g total fat (0.1g saturated fat); 25kJ (6 cal); 0.8g carbohydrate; 0.3g protein; 0.2g fibre*

**Beetroot dip can be made up to two days ahead; store, covered, in the refrigerator.**

# grilled fetta

200g fetta cheese
2 teaspoons olive oil
½ teaspoon sweet paprika
1 loaf ciabatta bread (440g), cut into 1cm slices
¼ cup (60ml) olive oil, extra
2 teaspoons coarsely chopped fresh
   oregano leaves

**1** Preheat grill.
**2** Pat cheese dry with absorbent paper. Place cheese on oven tray; brush top and sides with combined oil and paprika. Grill cheese until browned lightly.
**3** Lightly brush both sides of bread with extra oil. Toast bread on heated oiled grill plate (or grill or barbecue) until browned both sides.
**4** Sprinkle warm cheese with oregano; serve with toasted bread.

prep + cook time *20 minutes* serves *8*
nutritional count per serving *15.2g total fat (5.2g saturated fat); 1150kJ (275 cal); 24.7g carbohydrate; 9.1g protein; 1.6g fibre*

Any thick crusty-style bread can be used. Do not line oven tray with baking paper as it may burn during grilling.

# zucchini fritters with skordalia

4 medium zucchini (480g)

2 teaspoons coarse cooking salt

peanut oil, for deep-frying

**skordalia**

4 slices stale white sandwich bread (180g),
    crusts removed

4 cloves garlic, crushed

½ cup (125ml) olive oil

1 tablespoon lemon juice

1 tablespoon water, approximately

**batter**

1 cup (150g) self-raising flour

¾ cup (180ml) warm water

1 tablespoon olive oil

1 egg yolk

1  Make skordalia.

2  Cut zucchini into 1cm diagonal slices. Place zucchini in colander, sprinkle with salt; stand 30 minutes. Rinse zucchini under cold water; drain on absorbent paper.

3  Make batter.

4  Dip zucchini into batter, carefully lower into hot oil; cook zucchini until browned and crisp; drain on absorbent paper.

5  Serve zucchini fritters with skordalia.

**skordalia**  Briefly dip bread into a bowl of cold water, then gently squeeze out the water. Blend or process bread and garlic until combined. With motor operating, gradually add oil, juice and enough of the water, in a thin steady stream, until mixture is smooth and thick. Transfer to serving bowl.

**batter**  Sift flour into medium bowl; whisk in combined remaining ingredients until smooth. Stand batter 10 minutes. If batter thickens too much, whisk in a little extra water to give it a coating consistency.

**prep + cook  time** *1 hour (+ standing)* **serves** *6*
**nutritional count per serving**  *28g total fat (4.2g saturated fat); 1601kJ (383 cal); 26.5g carbohydrate; 5.4g protein; 3g fibre*

**Zucchini fritters are best made just before serving. Skordalia is best made on the day of serving; keep, covered, in the refrigerator.**

# labne

**You need 25cm piece cheesecloth for this recipe; it is available from fabric stores and some kitchenware shops.**

2 cups (560g) greek-style yogurt
1½ teaspoons fine table salt
1 tablespoon extra virgin olive oil
½ teaspoon dried chilli flakes
1 tablespoon coarsely chopped fresh coriander
1 tablespoon coarsely chopped fresh mint

**1** Combine yogurt and salt in medium bowl. Place a 12cm diameter strainer over bowl. Rinse cheesecloth in hot water; wring out then line strainer. Place yogurt into strainer; cover with plastic wrap. Refrigerate at least 24 hours to allow to drain.
**2** Turn labne onto serving plate, remove cheesecloth; drizzle labne with oil, sprinkle with chilli, coriander and mint.

**prep** *10 minutes (+ refrigeration)* **serves** *8*
**nutritional count per serving** *7.2g total fat (3.5g saturated fat); 439kJ (105 cal); 6.3g carbohydrate; 3.9g protein; 0g fibre*

**Labne can be drained longer than 24 hours, in fact, 48 hours is better; the longer it is drained the firmer it will become.**

# sardines with caper and parsley topping

8 sardines (360g), cleaned
⅓ cup (50g) self-raising flour
½ teaspoon sweet paprika
olive oil, for shallow-frying
**caper and parsley topping**
2 tablespoons rinsed, drained baby capers,
    chopped finely
1 clove garlic, crushed
¼ cup finely chopped fresh flat-leaf parsley
2 teaspoons finely grated lemon rind
2 teaspoons lemon juice

**1** Make caper and parsley topping.
**2** To butterfly sardines, cut through the underside
of the fish to the tail. Break backbone at tail; peel
away backbone. Trim sardines.
**3** Coat fish in combined flour and paprika; shake
away excess. Heat oil in large frying pan; shallow-fry
fish, in batches, until cooked through, drain on
absorbent paper.
**4** Sprinkle fish with caper and parsley topping.
Serve with lemon wedges, if you like.
**caper and parsley topping** Combine ingredients
in small bowl.

**prep + cook time** *45 minutes* **serves** *8*
**nutritional count per serving** *4.6g total fat*
*(0.9g saturated fat); 376kJ (90 cal);*
*4.8g carbohydrate; 7.1g protein; 0.5g fibre*

**The caper and parsley topping is best made
on the day of serving; store, covered, in the
refrigerator until ready to use.**

# mini baked herb ricotta

250g ricotta cheese

1 egg

1 tablespoon finely chopped fresh
    flat-leaf parsley

1 teaspoon finely chopped fresh thyme

1 clove garlic, crushed

**1** Preheat oven to 180°C/160°C fan-forced. Oil
18 holes of two 12-hole (1½-tablespoons/20ml)
mini muffin pans.

**2** Blend or process ingredients until smooth.
Divide mixture among pan holes. Bake about
20 minutes or until browned lightly.

**prep + cook time** *30 minutes* **makes** *18*
**nutritional count per ricotta** *1.9g total fat
(1.1g saturated fat); 105kJ (25 cal);
0.2g carbohydrate; 1.8g protein; 0g fibre*

**Serve mini baked ricottas warm or cold.
Recipe can be made a day ahead; store,
covered, in the refrigerator.**

# chilli tomato

¼ cup coarsely chopped fresh flat-leaf parsley
2 cloves garlic, crushed
½ teaspoon dried chilli flakes
2 tablespoons olive oil
4 large egg tomatoes (360g), sliced thickly

1 Combine parsley, garlic and chilli in small bowl.
2 Heat oil in large frying pan, carefully add tomato in a single layer; cook, over high heat, 2 minutes. Turn tomato, sprinkle with parsley mixture; cook, shaking pan occasionally, about 1 minute or until tomato is caramelised but still holding its shape.
3 Transfer to serving plate; drizzle with pan juices.

prep + cook time *15 minutes* serves *6*
nutritional count per serving *6.2g total fat (0.9g saturated fat); 276kJ (66 cal); 1.5g carbohydrate; 0.7g protein; 1.1g fibre*

Take care when adding tomato to pan as it may splatter. Tomato is best cooked just before serving.

# mini chicken souvlakia

**1kg chicken thigh fillets**
**2 tablespoons olive oil**
**2 tablespoons lemon juice**
**⅓ cup finely chopped fresh mint**
**2 cloves garlic, crushed**
**1½ teaspoons smoked paprika**

**1** Trim any fat from chicken; cut chicken into 2cm thick strips. Combine chicken in medium bowl with remaining ingredients. Thread chicken onto 20 bamboo skewers; cover, refrigerate 3 hours or overnight.
**2** Cook skewers on heated oiled grill plate (or grill or barbecue) until browned and cooked through. Serve with lemon wedges, if you like.

**prep + cook time** *35 minutes*
*(+ refrigeration)* **makes** *20*
**nutritional count per skewer** *5.4g total fat (1.4g saturated fat); 364kJ (87 cal); 0.1g carbohydrate; 9.4g protein; 0.1g fibre*

**Soak the skewers in cold water for at least an hour before using to prevent them from scorching during cooking.**
**For optimum flavour, marinate the chicken overnight.**

# lemon pepper squid

500g squid hoods
½ cup (75g) plain flour
2 tablespoons lemon pepper
2 teaspoons dried rigani
1 teaspoon coarse cooking salt
peanut oil, for deep-frying
1 tablespoon coarsely chopped fresh parsley

**1** Cut squid down centre to open out; score inside in diagonal pattern then cut into thick strips.
**2** Combine flour, lemon pepper, rigani and salt in large bowl; add squid, toss to coat in mixture, shake away excess.
**3** Heat oil in medium saucepan; deep-fry squid, in batches, until tender. Drain on absorbent paper. Serve sprinkled with parsley.

**prep + cook time** *30 minutes* **serves** *4*
**nutritional count per serving** *8.1g total fat (1.7g saturated fat); 953kJ (228 cal); 14.4g carbohydrate; 23.3g protein; 1.7g fibre*

**Lemon pepper is available from the dried herb and spice section at most supermarkets. If you use one containing salt, reduce the salt quantity in this recipe.**

# turkish lamb fillo cigars

2 tablespoons olive oil

1 medium brown onion (150g), chopped finely

2 cloves garlic, crushed

2 teaspoons ground allspice

2 teaspoons ground coriander

1½ teaspoons ground cinnamon

1 teaspoon ground cumin

300g lean lamb mince

1 tablespoon lemon juice

6 sheets fillo pastry

100g butter, melted

**mint yogurt**

½ cup (140g) greek-style yogurt

1 tablespoon finely chopped fresh mint

**1**  Heat oil in medium frying pan, add onion and garlic; cook, stirring, until onion softens. Add spices; cook, stirring, until fragrant. Add mince; cook, stirring until mince is cooked through. Stir in juice; cool.

**2**  Preheat oven to 220°C/200°C fan-forced. Oil oven tray; line with baking paper.

**3**  Brush 1 sheet of pastry with butter; top with two more sheets, brushing each with butter. Cut layered sheets into 8 rectangles. Press 1 tablespoon of lamb mixture into a log shape along one long end of each rectangle. Roll pastry over filling; fold in sides then roll up to form a cigar shape. Repeat to make a total of 16 cigar shapes.

**4**  Place cigars, about 2cm apart, on oven tray, brush with remaining butter. Bake about 15 minutes or until browned lightly.

**5**  Meanwhile, make mint yogurt.

**6**  Serve warm cigars with mint yogurt.

**mint yogurt**  Combine ingredients in small bowl.

**prep + cook time** *1 hour 30 minutes*  **makes** *16*
**nutritional count per piece** *9.4g total fat (4.7g saturated fat); 510kJ (122 cal); 4.3g carbohydrate; 5g protein; 0.3g fibre*

**To prevent pastry from drying out, cover with plastic wrap then top with a damp tea-towel until ready to use.**
**Uncooked fillo cigars are suitable to freeze.**

# broad bean dip

500g frozen broad beans

1 clove garlic, crushed

1 teaspoon ground cumin

½ teaspoon smoked paprika

2 tablespoons olive oil

1 tablespoon lemon juice

1 tablespoon finely chopped fresh mint

1 tablespoon olive oil, extra

¼ teaspoon smoked paprika, extra

**1** Cook beans in medium saucepan of boiling water until tender; drain, reserving some of the cooking liquid. When cool enough to handle, peel away grey-coloured outer shells from beans.

**2** Blend or process beans with garlic, spices, oil, juice, mint and enough of the reserved cooking liquid until mixture is smooth.

**3** Serve dip drizzled with extra oil and sprinkled with extra paprika.

**prep + cook time** *20 minutes* **makes** *1¾ cups*
**nutritional count per teaspoon** *0.7g total fat (0.1g saturated fat); 29kJ (7 cal); 0.1g carbohydrate; 0.2g protein; 0.2g fibre*

**Dip can be made a day ahead; store, covered, in the refrigerator.**

# char-grilled banana chillies

4 red banana chillies (500g)
1 tablespoon white wine vinegar
1 tablespoon olive oil
2 teaspoons finely chopped fresh flat-leaf parsley

1 Preheat grill.
2 Cook whole chillies under hot grill until blistered and blackened. Cover chillies with plastic or paper for 5 minutes; peel away skin.
3 Arrange whole chillies on serving plate; drizzle with combined vinegar, oil and parsley.

prep + cook time *30 minutes* serves *4*
nutritional count per serving *4.8g total fat (0.6g saturated fat); 238kJ (57 cal); 2.1g carbohydrate; 0.8g protein; 1.4g fibre*

Recipe can be made a day ahead; store, covered, in the refrigerator.

109

# dolmades

2 tablespoons olive oil

2 medium brown onions (300g), chopped finely

150g lean lamb mince

¾ cup (150g) white long-grain rice

2 tablespoons pine nuts

½ cup finely chopped fresh flat-leaf parsley

2 tablespoons finely chopped fresh dill

2 tablespoons finely chopped fresh mint

2 tablespoons lemon juice

1 cup (250ml) water

500g preserved vine leaves

1 cup (250ml) water, extra

1 tablespoon lemon juice, extra

¾ cup (200g) yogurt

**1** Heat oil in large saucepan, add onion; cook, stirring, until softened. Add mince; cook, stirring, until mince is browned. Stir in rice and pine nuts. Add herbs, juice and the water. Bring to the boil; reduce heat, simmer, covered, about 10 minutes or until water is absorbed and rice is partially cooked. Cool.

**2** Rinse vine leaves in cold water. Drop leaves into a large saucepan of boiling water, in batches, for a few seconds, transfer to colander; rinse under cold water, drain well.

**3** Place a vine leaf, smooth side down on bench, trim large stem. Place a heaped teaspoon of rice mixture in centre. Fold stem end and sides over filling; roll up firmly. Line medium heavy-based saucepan with a few vine leaves, place rolls, close together, seam side down on leaves.

**4** Pour the extra water over top of rolls; cover rolls with any remaining vine leaves. Place a plate on top of the leaves to keep rolls under the water during cooking. Cover pan tightly, bring to the boil; reduce heat, simmer, over very low heat, 1½ hours. Remove from heat; stand, covered about 2 hours or until all the liquid has been absorbed.

**5** Serve with combined extra juice and yogurt.

**prep + cook time** *3 hours*
*(+ standing)* **serves** *10*
**nutritional count per serving** *7.6g total fat (1.6g saturated fat); 690kJ (165 cal); 14.9g carbohydrate; 7.7g protein; 3.2g fibre*

**Use any torn or damaged leaves to line the base of the pan and to cover the rolls. If you don't have enough vine leaves to cover the rolls in the pan, use a circle of baking paper, then top with the plate. Dolmades are best made a day ahead; store, covered, in the refrigerator.**

# mini felafel with tomato salsa

400g can chickpeas, rinsed, drained
1 small white onion (80g), chopped finely
½ cup finely chopped fresh flat-leaf parsley
2 tablespoons finely chopped fresh coriander
2 teaspoons ground cumin
2 teaspoons ground coriander
1 tablespoon finely grated lemon rind
1 teaspoon salt
¼ cup (35g) plain flour
peanut oil, for deep-frying
**tomato salsa**
1 medium egg tomato (75g), chopped finely
1 tablespoon coarsely chopped fresh coriander
1 tablespoon olive oil

**1** To make felafel, blend or process chickpeas, onion, herbs, spices, rind and salt until coarsely chopped. Add flour; process until mixture forms a paste. Transfer mixture to medium bowl; cover, refrigerate 1 hour.
**2** Make tomato salsa.
**3** Shape felafel mixture between two teaspoons into oval shapes. Heat oil in medium deep frying pan; cook felafel, in batches, until browned. Drain on absorbent paper.
**4** Serve felafel with tomato salsa.
**tomato salsa** Combine ingredients in small bowl.

**prep + cook time** *1 hour 30 minutes (+ refrigeration)* **makes 32**
**nutritional count per serving** *1.4g total fat (0.2g saturated fat); 105kJ (25 cal); 2.1g carbohydrate; 0.7g protein; 0.6g fibre*

**Felafel can be made a day ahead; store, covered, in the refrigerator.**

# greek meatballs

1 tablespoon olive oil
1 medium brown onion (150g), chopped finely
2 cloves garlic, crushed
1kg lean lamb mince
1 egg
1½ cups (100g) stale breadcrumbs
2 tablespoons lemon juice
¼ cup finely chopped fresh flat-leaf parsley
¼ cup finely chopped fresh mint
⅓ cup (50g) plain flour
olive oil, extra, for shallow-frying

**1** Heat oil in medium frying pan, add onion and garlic; cook, stirring, until onion is softened. Cool.
**2** Combine onion mixture with mince, egg, breadcrumbs, juice, parsley and mint in large bowl. Cover, refrigerate 1 hour.
**3** Roll level tablespoons of mixture into balls; toss balls in flour, shake away excess. Heat extra oil in same cleaned pan; shallow-fry meatballs, in batches, until cooked through. Drain on absorbent paper.
**4** Serve meatballs with yogurt, if you like.

**prep + cook time** *1 hour*
*(+ refrigeration)* **makes** *50*
**nutritional count per meatball** *4.7g total fat (1.1g saturated fat); 297kJ (71 cal); 2.3g carbohydrate; 4.7g protein; 0.2g fibre*

**The oil should be very hot before cooking the meatballs.**
**Beef or veal mince can also be used in this recipe.**

# glossary

ALLSPICE also known as pimento or jamaican pepper; a berry, so-named because it tastes like a combination of nutmeg, cumin, clove and cinnamon. Also available ground.

ALMONDS flat, pointy-ended nuts with a pitted brown shell enclosing a creamy white kernel that is covered by a brown skin.

flaked paper-thin slices.

slivered thin lengthways-cut pieces.

ARTICHOKE, GLOBE the bud of a large plant from the thistle family; has tough, petal-shaped leaves and an inedible prickly choke that should be discarded leaving the tender artichoke heart. Artichoke hearts are also available, packed in brine in cans or in glass jars.

BASIL an aromatic herb; there are many types, but the most commonly used is sweet, or common, basil.

BEANS

broad also known as fava, windsor and horse beans. Fresh and frozen forms should be peeled twice, discarding the outer long green pod and the tough beige-green inner shell.

white in this book, some recipes may simply call for 'white beans', a generic term we use for cannellini, haricot, navy or great northern beans – all of which can be substituted for each other.

BEETROOT also known as red beets or beets; a firm, round root vegetable.

BREAD

brioche can be made in the shape of a loaf or roll. A rich, French yeast bread with a dark, golden, flaky crust; typically baked in a fluted pan.

ciabatta in italian, the word means 'slipper', which is the traditional shape of this white bread with a crisp crust.

croissant the French word for crescent. A rich, flaky pastry breakfast roll shaped as a crescent with a crisp texture on the outside, and a flaky layered soft buttery centre.

french stick a long, narrow cylindrical loaf. It usually has a crisp brown crust and light chewy centre. A standard stick is 5-6cm wide and 3-4cm tall, but can be up to a metre in length. Also known as french bread, french loaf or baguette.

pide see bread, turkish.

pitta also known as lebanese bread; a pocket bread sold in large, flat pieces that separate into two thin rounds. Also available in small thick pieces called pocket pitta.

sourdough made by using a small amount of 'starter dough', i.e., dough from a previous batch, containing a yeast culture. Part of the resulting dough is then saved to use as the starter dough next time.

turkish also known as pide; comes in long (about 45cm) flat loaves as well as individual rounds. Made from wheat flour and sprinkled with sesame seeds or kalonji (black onion seeds).

BREADCRUMBS

packaged fine-textured, crunchy, purchased white breadcrumbs.

stale one- or two-day-old bread made into crumbs by blending or processing.

BUTTER use salted or unsalted (sweet) butter; 125g is equal to one stick (4oz).

CAPERBERRIES fruit formed after the caper buds have flowered; caperberries are pickled, usually with stalks intact.

CAPERS the grey-green buds of a warm climate (usually Mediterranean) shrub; sold either dried and salted or pickled in a vinegar brine. Baby capers, those picked early, are smaller, fuller-flavoured and more expensive than the full-sized ones. Capers should be rinsed well before using.

CAPSICUM also known as bell pepper or, simply, pepper. Comes in many colours: red, green, yellow, orange and purplish-black. Discard seeds and membranes before use.

vine-sweet minicaps can be orange, red or yellow and are about the size of baby red capsicums. Flavoursome with a crispy texture; they have a very fine skin, but still need deseeding.

CAYENNE PEPPER a long, thin-fleshed, extremely hot red chilli usually sold dried and ground.

CHEESE

blue mould-treated cheeses mottled with blue veining. Varieties include firm and crumbly stilton types to mild, creamy brie-like cheeses.

bocconcini baby mozzarella; walnut-sized, delicate, semi-soft, white cheese. Spoils rapidly so must be kept under refrigeration, in brine, for 2 days at most.

cream cheese also known as Philly or Philadelphia, a soft, cows-milk cheese.

fetta a crumbly textured goat or sheep milk cheese with a sharp, salty taste.

goats made from goat milk; has an earthy, strong taste. Available as soft and firm, and in various shapes and sizes, sometimes rolled in ash or herbs.

haloumi a firm, cream-coloured sheep-milk cheese matured in brine; can be grilled or fried, briefly, without breaking down. Should be eaten while still warm as it becomes tough and rubbery on cooling.

manchego sharp, firm, spanish cheese; found in most specialty food stores. Parmesan cheese may be substituted if manchego is not available.

mascarpone a cultured cream product made in much the same way as yogurt. It's a buttery-rich, cream-like cheese made from cows milk. Ivory-coloured, soft and delicate, with the texture of softened butter,

mozzarella a soft, spun-curd cheese. It has a low melting point and wonderfully elastic texture when heated, and is used to add texture rather than flavour.

ricotta the name for this soft, white, cows-milk cheese roughly translates as 'cooked again'. It's made from whey, a by-product of other cheese-making, to which fresh milk and acid are added. Ricotta is a sweet, moist cheese with a slightly grainy texture.

romano a hard cheese with excellent keeping qualities. Made from sheep milk, this straw-coloured cheese has a grainy texture and is mainly used for grating. Substitute with parmesan.

parmesan also known as parmigiano; a hard, grainy, cows-milk cheese. The curd is salted in brine for a month before being aged for up to two years in humid conditions.

CHERVIL also known as cicily; a herb with a mild fennel flavour.

CHICKPEAS also called garbanzos, hummus or channa; an irregularly round, sandy-coloured legume.

CHILLI available in many types and sizes: generally, the smaller the chilli the hotter it is. Use rubber gloves when seeding and chopping fresh chillies as they can burn your skin. Removing seeds and membranes lessens the heat level.

banana also known as wax chillies or hungarian peppers; are almost as mild as capsicum but have a distinctively sweet sharpness to their taste. Sold in varying degrees of ripeness, they can be found in pale olive green, yellow and red varieties at greengrocers and most supermarkets.

flakes dried, deep-red, dehydrated chilli slices and whole seeds.

long red available both fresh and dried; a generic term used for any moderately hot, long (6cm to 8cm), thin chilli.

thai red also known as 'scuds'; small, very hot and bright red in colour.

CHORIZO a sausage of Spanish origin, made of coarsely ground pork and highly seasoned with garlic and chillies.

COPPA a salted dried sausage made from the neck or shoulder of pork. Is deep red in colour and can be found in both mild and spicy versions.

CORIANDER also known as pak chee, cilantro or chinese parsley; a bright-green leafy herb with a pungent flavour. Stems and roots of coriander may also be used; wash well before chopping. Coriander is also available ground or as seeds, but these are no substitute for fresh coriander as the tastes are very different.

CREAM we used fresh cream, also known as pure cream and pouring cream, unless otherwise stated. It has no additives, unlike thickened cream. Minimum fat content 35%.

sour a thick, cultured soured cream. Minimum fat content 35%.

crème fraîche mature fermented cream having a slightly tangy, nutty flavour and velvety texture. Minimum fat content 35%.

CUMIN also known as zeera or comino.

EGGPLANT purple-skinned vegetable also known as aubergine. Can also be purchased char-grilled, packed in oil, in jars.

FENNEL also known as finocchio or anise; a white to very pale green-white, firm, crisp, roundish vegetable about 8-12cm in diameter. The bulb has a slightly sweet, anise flavour but the leaves (fronds) have a much stronger taste. Also the name given to dried seeds having a licorice flavour.

FISH FILLETS, FIRM WHITE any firm white boneless fish fillet – blue eye, bream, swordfish, ling, whiting or sea perch are all good choices. Check for any small pieces of bone in the fillets and use tweezers to remove them.

FLOUR

plain an all-purpose flour made from wheat.

rice a very fine flour made from ground white rice.

self-raising plain flour sifted with baking powder in the proportion of 1 cup flour to 2 teaspoons baking powder.

GHEE also known as clarified butter; butter that has had its milk solids removed, so it can be heated to a high temperature without burning.

HARISSA a moroccan sauce or paste made from dried chillies, cumin, garlic, oil and caraway seeds. Is available from Middle-Eastern food stores and major supermarkets.

LEBANESE CUCUMBER short, slender and thin-skinned. Probably the most popular variety because of its tender, edible skin, tiny, yielding seeds and sweet, fresh taste.

LEMON PEPPER also known as lemon pepper seasoning, a blend of crushed black pepper, lemon, herbs and spices. Is available from the dried herb and spice section at most supermarkets.

LETTUCE, BABY COS also known as romaine lettuce; the traditional caesar salad lettuce. Long, with leaves ranging from dark green on the outside to almost white near the core; the leaves have a stiff centre rib that gives a slight cupping effect to the leaf.

MINCE also known as ground meat.

MUSHROOMS, BUTTON small, cultivated white mushrooms having a delicate, subtle flavour.

MUSSELS buy from a fish market where there is reliably fresh fish; must be tightly closed when bought, indicating they are alive. Before cooking, scrub the shells with a strong brush and remove the beards; discard any shells that do not open after cooking. Varieties include black and green-lip.

MUSTARD, WHOLEGRAIN also known as seeded. A french-style coarse-grain mustard made from crushed mustard seeds and dijon-style french mustard.

OIL

cooking spray we use a cholesterol-free cooking spray made from canola oil.

olive made from ripened olives. Extra virgin and virgin are the best, while extra light or light refers to taste not fat levels.

vegetable sourced from plants rather than animal fats.

OLIVES

anchovy-stuffed green manzanilla medium-sized green or black pickled olives; found at specialty food stores.

fetta-stuffed green green olives stuffed with fetta cheese.

green those harvested before fully ripened and are, as a rule, denser and more bitter than their black relatives.

kalamata small, sharp-tasting, brine-cured black olives.

ligurian very small black olives with a nutty flavour.

niçoise small black olives.

pimiento-stuffed green a green olive with a lively, briny bitterness and stuffed with a morsel of capsicum, which adds a flash of colour.

sicilian dark olive green in colour; can be found almost everywhere olives are sold. Crack but do not seed them, and make certain to alert your guests to the seeds. Brine-cured sicilian olives are smooth and fine-skinned, crisp and crunchy to the bite – they have a refreshingly piquant, buttery flavour.

wild available from select delicatessens. Substitute with small ligurian olives if you can't find them.

ONION

green also scallion or, incorrectly, shallot; an immature onion picked before the bulb has formed, having a long, bright-green edible stalk.

red also known as spanish, red spanish or bermuda onion; a sweet-flavoured, large, purple-red onion.

shallots also called french shallots, golden shallots or eschalots; small, brown-skinned, elongated members of the onion family. Grows in tight clusters similar to garlic.

spring onions with small white bulbs and long narrow, green leafy tops.

PANCETTA pork belly that is cured but not smoked; bacon can be substituted.

PAPRIKA ground dried sweet red capsicum (bell pepper); there are many types available, including sweet, hot, mild and smoked.

PARSLEY, FLAT-LEAF also known as continental or italian parsley.

PEPPERCORNS, BLACK picked when the berry is not quite ripe, then dried until it shrivels and the skin turns dark brown to black. Strongly flavoured.

PINE NUTS also known as pignoli; not, in fact, a nut but a small, cream-coloured kernel from pine cones.

PISTACHIO pale green, delicately flavoured nut inside hard off-white shells. To peel, soak shelled nuts in boiling water for about 5 minutes; drain, then pat dry with absorbent paper. Rub skins with a cloth to peel.

POLENTA also known as cornmeal; a flour-like cereal made of dried corn (maize). Also the name of the dish made from it.

POMEGRANATE MOLASSES is thicker, browner and more concentrated in flavour than grenadine, the sweet, red pomegranate syrup used in cocktails. Has a tart, fruity quality similar to balsamic vinegar. It is available from Middle-Eastern food stores, specialty food shops and better delicatessens.

POTATOES, BABY NEW also known as chats; not a separate variety but an early harvest with very thin skin.

PRAWNS also known as shrimp.

PROSCIUTTO cured, air-dried, pressed ham. Usually sold thinly sliced.

QUAIL small, delicately flavoured, domestically grown game birds ranging in weight from 250g to 300g; also known as partridge.

QUINCE yellow-skinned fruit with a hard texture and an astringent, tart taste; eaten cooked or as a preserve.

RADISH a peppery root vegetable related to the mustard plant. The small round red variety is the mildest.

RAISINS dried sweet grapes.

RICE

arborio small, round-grain rice, well-suited to absorb a large amount of liquid; especially suitable for risottos.

long-grain elongated grain, remains separate when cooked; most popular steaming rice in South-East Asia.

medium-grain previously sold as Calrose rice; extremely versatile rice that can be substituted for short- or long-grain rice if necessary.

short-grain a fat, almost round-grain rice with a high starch content; tends to clump together when cooked.

RIGANI, DRIED a type of oregano but with a stronger flavour; used in many Greek dishes. Available from specialty supermarkets and delicatessens. If unavailable, use dried oregano.

ROASTING NUTS put shelled nuts in a baking pan and bake in a hot oven, stirring occasionally, until slightly golden in colour, about 10 minutes.

ROCKET also known as arugula, rugula and rucola; a peppery-tasting green leaf. Baby rocket leaves, also known as wild rocket, are both smaller and less peppery.

ROCKMELON also known as cantaloupe and musk melon. Has a lovely, moist, sweet orange flesh.

ROSEWATER called gulab in India. An extract made from crushed rose petals; used for its aromatic quality in many sweetmeats and desserts. Available from Middle-Eastern food stores and some delicatessens.

SAFFRON available in strands or ground form; imparts a yellow-orange colour to food once infused. Quality varies greatly; the best is the most expensive spice in the world. Should be stored in the freezer.

SASHIMI skinless, boneless raw fish pieces certified as safe to eat. Use the freshest, sashimi-quality fish you can find. Raw fish sold as sashimi has to meet stringent guidelines regarding its handling and treatment after leaving the water. We suggest you seek local advice from authorities before eating any raw seafood.

SCALLOPS a bivalve mollusc with a fluted shell valve.

SESAME SEEDS black and white are the most common of this small oval seed, however, there are red and brown varieties also.

SOPRESSA a semi-hard pork salami typically flavoured with pepper, cloves, cinnamon, nutmeg, rosemary and garlic. Can be hot or mild.

SPECK also known as cured pork.

SPINACH also known as english spinach and, incorrectly, silver beet.

SQUID a type of mollusc; also known as calamari. Buy squid hoods to make preparation easier.

STERILISING JARS place cleaned glass jars on their sides in a large saucepan; cover with cold water. Cover pan, bring to the boil, and boil for 20 minutes. Carefully remove jars from water; drain. Stand jars, top-side up, on a wooden board. The heat from the jars will cause any remaining water to evaporate quickly. Place jars, on wooden board, in a cold oven (do not allow the jars to touch); heat oven temperature to very slow (120°C/100°C fan-forced), then leave jars in oven for 30 minutes. Plastic screw-top lids give a good seal (plastic snap-on lids are not airtight enough). Plastic lids must be well washed, rinsed and dried, or put through the dishwasher.

SUGAR

brown an extremely soft, finely granulated sugar retaining molasses for its characteristic colour and flavour.

caster also known as superfine or finely granulated table sugar.

SUMAC a purple-red, astringent spice ground from berries growing on shrubs that flourish wild around the Mediterranean; adds a tart, lemony flavour to dips and dressings.

TOMATO

pasta sauce, bottled a prepared sauce made from a blend of tomatoes, herbs and spices.

paste triple-concentrated tomato purée used to flavour soups, stews, sauces and casseroles.

VEAL SCHNITZELS a thinly sliced steak available crumbed or plain (uncrumbed); we use plain schnitzel, sometimes called escalopes, in our recipes, unless indicated otherwise.

VINE LEAVES from early spring, fresh grapevine leaves can be found in most specialist greengrocers. Alternatively, cryovac-packed leaves in brine can be found in Middle-Eastern food shops and some delicatessens; these must be rinsed well and dried before using. We used vine leaves in brine; available in jars and packets from supermarkets.

VINEGAR

balsamic made from trebbiano grapes; it is a deep rich brown colour with a sweet and sour flavour.

cider (apple cider) made from crushed fermented apples.

red wine based on fermented red wine.

sherry made from a blend of wines and left in wood vats to mature, where they develop a rich mellow flavour.

white made from cane sugar.

white wine made from white wine.

WATERCRESS also known as winter rocket; one of the cress family, a large group of peppery greens. Highly perishable, so must be used as soon as possible after purchase.

WITLOF also known as chicory or belgian endive; its cigar-shaped, tightly packed heads have pale, yellow-green tips, and a delicately bitter flavour. Eaten cooked or raw.

YEAST a 7g (¼oz) sachet of dried yeast (2 teaspoons) is equal to 15g (½oz) compressed yeast; they can be substituted for each other.

YOGURT we used plain, unflavoured yogurt, unless otherwise specified.

ZUCCHINI also known as courgette; small, pale- or dark-green, yellow or white vegetable belonging to the squash family. Harvested when young, its edible flowers can be stuffed then deep-fried or oven-baked to make a delicious appetiser.

# conversion chart

## MEASURES

One Australian metric measuring cup holds approximately 250ml; one Australian metric tablespoon holds 20ml; one Australian metric teaspoon holds 5ml.

The difference between one country's measuring cups and another's is within a two- or three-teaspoon variance, and will not affect your cooking results. North America, New Zealand and the United Kingdom use a 15ml tablespoon.

All cup and spoon measurements are level. The most accurate way of measuring dry ingredients is to weigh them. When measuring liquids, use a clear glass or plastic jug with the metric markings.

We use large eggs with an average weight of 60g.

## DRY MEASURES

| METRIC | IMPERIAL |
|---|---|
| 15g | ½oz |
| 30g | 1oz |
| 60g | 2oz |
| 90g | 3oz |
| 125g | 4oz (¼lb) |
| 155g | 5oz |
| 185g | 6oz |
| 220g | 7oz |
| 250g | 8oz (½lb) |
| 280g | 9oz |
| 315g | 10oz |
| 345g | 11oz |
| 375g | 12oz (¾lb) |
| 410g | 13oz |
| 440g | 14oz |
| 470g | 15oz |
| 500g | 16oz (1lb) |
| 750g | 24oz (1½lb) |
| 1kg | 32oz (2lb) |

## LIQUID MEASURES

| METRIC | IMPERIAL |
|---|---|
| 30ml | 1 fluid oz |
| 60ml | 2 fluid oz |
| 100ml | 3 fluid oz |
| 125ml | 4 fluid oz |
| 150ml | 5 fluid oz (¼ pint/1 gill) |
| 190ml | 6 fluid oz |
| 250ml | 8 fluid oz |
| 300ml | 10 fluid oz (½ pint) |
| 500ml | 16 fluid oz |
| 600ml | 20 fluid oz (1 pint) |
| 1000ml (1 litre) | 1¾ pints |

## LENGTH MEASURES

| METRIC | IMPERIAL |
|---|---|
| 3mm | ⅛in |
| 6mm | ¼in |
| 1cm | ½in |
| 2cm | ¾in |
| 2.5cm | 1in |
| 5cm | 2in |
| 6cm | 2½in |
| 8cm | 3in |
| 10cm | 4in |
| 13cm | 5in |
| 15cm | 6in |
| 18cm | 7in |
| 20cm | 8in |
| 23cm | 9in |
| 25cm | 10in |
| 28cm | 11in |
| 30cm | 12in (1ft) |

## OVEN TEMPERATURES

These oven temperatures are only a guide for conventional ovens. For fan-forced ovens, check the manufacturer's manual.

| | °C (CELSIUS) | °F (FAHRENHEIT) | GAS MARK |
|---|---|---|---|
| Very slow | 120 | 250 | ½ |
| Slow | 150 | 275-300 | 1-2 |
| Moderately slow | 160 | 325 | 3 |
| Moderate | 180 | 350-375 | 4-5 |
| Moderately hot | 200 | 400 | 6 |
| Hot | 220 | 425-450 | 7-8 |
| Very hot | 240 | 475 | 9 |

# index

**ACP BOOKS**
**General manager** Christine Whiston
**Editorial director** Susan Tomnay
**Creative director & designer** Hieu Chi Nguyen
**Art director** Hannah Blackmore
**Senior editor** Wendy Bryant
**Food director** Pamela Clark
**Test Kitchen manager + nutritional information** Belinda Farlow
**Recipe development** Clara Luboff, Rebecca Squadrito, Louise Patniotis
**Director of sales** Brian Cearnes
**Marketing manager** Bridget Cody
**Communications & brand manager** Xanthe Roberts
**Senior business analyst** Rebecca Varela
**Circulation manager** Jarna Mclean
**Operations manager** David Scotto
**Production manager** Victoria Jefferys
**European rights enquiries** Laura Bamford  lbamford@acpuk.com

ACP Books are published by ACP Magazines a division of PBL Media Pty Limited
**Group publishing & sales director, Women's lifestyle** Lynette Phillips
**Group editorial director, Women's lifestyle** Pat Ingram
**Commercial manager, Women's lifestyle** Seymour Cohen
**Marketing director, Women's lifestyle** Matthew Dominello
**Research director, Women's lifestyle** Justin Stone
**PBL Media, Chief Executive Officer** Ian Law

**Produced by** ACP Books, Sydney.

**Published by** ACP Books, a division of ACP Magazines Ltd,
54 Park St, Sydney; GPO Box 4088, Sydney, NSW 2001.
phone (02) 9282 8618; fax (02) 9267 9438.
acpbooks@acpmagazines.com.au; www.acpbooks.com.au

**Printed by** Dai Nippon in Korea.

**Australia** Distributed by Network Services,
phone +61 2 9282 8777; fax +61 2 9264 3278;
networkweb@networkservicescompany.com.au
**United Kingdom** Distributed by Australian Consolidated Press (UK),
phone (01604) 642 200; fax (01604) 642 300; books@acpuk.com
**New Zealand** Distributed by Netlink Distribution Company,
phone (9) 366 9966; ask@ndc.co.nz
**South Africa** Distributed by PSD Promotions,
phone (27 11) 392 6065/6/7; fax (27 11) 392 6079/80; orders@psdprom.co.za
**Canada** Distributed by Publishers Group Canada
phone (800) 663 5714; fax (800) 565 3770; service@raincoast.com

Title: Tapas bar / compiler, Pamela Clark.
ISBN: 978 1 86396 862 1 (pbk.)
Notes: Includes index.
Subjects: Tapas. Appetizers. Cookery, Spanish.
Other Authors/Contributors: Clark, Pamela.
Dewey Number: 641.812
© ACP Magazines Ltd 2009
ABN 18 053 273 546
This publication is copyright. No part of it may be reproduced or transmitted
in any form without the written permission of the publishers.

Scanpan cookware is used in the AWW Test Kitchen.

The publishers would like to thank the following for props used in photography:
Alfresco Emporium, Chee Soon & Fitzgerald, Hub Furniture, Mud Australia,
Papaya, Teranova Tile Boutique, Thonet Australia, Village Living Pty Ltd.

**Send recipe enquiries to: recipeenquiries@acpmagazines.com.au**